P9-DFT-465

WORLD RELIGIONS
ISLAM
FOURTH EDITION

WORLD RELIGIONS

WORLD RELIGIONS
ISLAM
FOURTH EDITION

by
Matthew S. Gordon
Series Editors: Joanne O'Brien and Martin Palmer

CHELSEA HOUSE
PUBLISHERS
An imprint of Infobase Publishing

Islam, Fourth Edition

Chelsea House
An imprint of Infobase Publishing
132 West 31st Street
New York NY 10001

Library of Congress Cataloging-in-Publication Data
Gordon, Matthew.
 Islam / by Matthew Gordon. -- 4th ed.
     p. cm. — (World religions)
 Includes bibliographical references and index.
 ISBN 978-1-60413-109-3
 1. Islam—Juvenile literature. I. Title. II. Series
 BL161.3.G669 2009
 297—dc22

                    2008035810

Chelsea House books are available at special discounts when purchased in bulk quantities for businesses, associations, institutions, or sales promotions. Please call our Special Sales Department in New York at (212) 967-8800 or (800) 322-8755.

You can find Chelsea House on the World Wide Web at http://www.chelseahouse.com

This book was produced for Chelsea House by Bender Richardson White, Uxbridge, U.K.
Project Editor: Lionel Bender
Text Editor: Ronne Randall
Designer: Ben White
Picture Researchers: Joanne O'Brien and Kim Richardson
Maps and symbols: Stefan Chabluk

Printed in China

CP BRW 10 9 8 7 6 5 4 3 2 1

This book is printed on acid-free paper.

All links and Web addresses were checked and verified to be correct at the time of publication. Because of the dynamic nature of the Web, some addresses and links may have changed since publication and may no longer be valid.

CONTENTS

PREFACE

Almost from the start of civilization, more than 10,000 years ago, religion has shaped human history. Today more than half the world's population practice a major religion or indigenous spiritual tradition. In many 21st-century societies, including the United States, religion still shapes people's lives and plays a key role in politics and culture. And in societies throughout the world increasing ethnic and cultural diversity has led to a variety of religions being practiced side by side. This makes it vital that we understand as much as we can about the world's religions.

The World Religions series, of which this book is a part, sets out to achieve this aim. It is written and designed to appeal to both students and general readers. The books offer clear, accessible overviews of the major religious traditions and institutions of our time. Each volume in the series describes where a particular religion is practiced, its origins and history, its central beliefs and important rituals, and its contributions to world civilization. Carefully chosen photographs complement the text, and sidebars, a map, fact file, glossary, bibliography, and index are included to help readers gain a more complete understanding of the subject at hand.

These books will help clarify what religion is all about and reveal both the similarities and differences in the great spiritual traditions practiced around the world today.

Current Muslim Population

- 90% and over
- 50%–89%
- 10%–49%
- 0%–9%

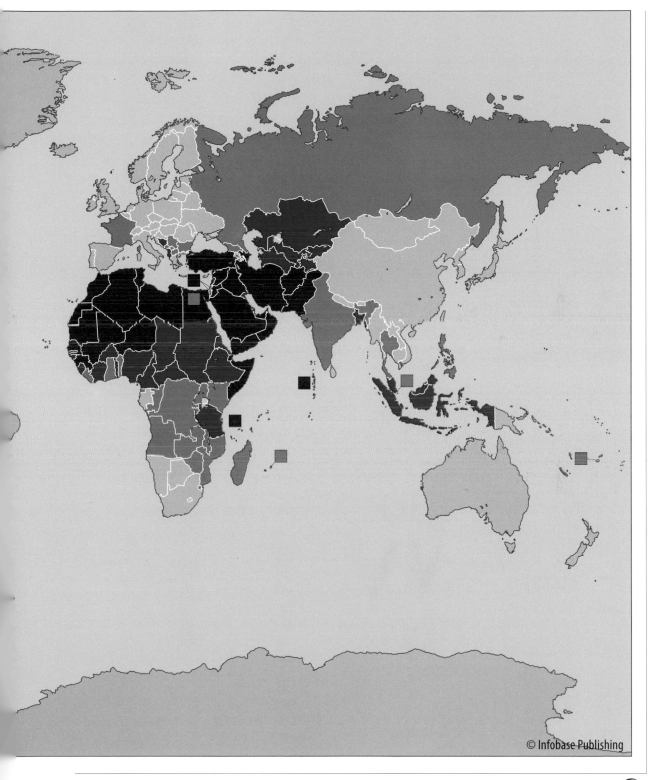

CHAPTER 1

INTRODUCTION: THE MODERN ISLAMIC WORLD

Islam, one of the most widespread religions in the world, is second only to Christianity in number of followers. The people who believe in the principles of Islam and practice its rituals are called Muslims, and they make up a large segment of the world population. Of the roughly 6.5 billion people in the world, around 1.4 billion are Muslims.

On the continents of Africa and Asia and in the area known as the Middle East, Islam is the dominant religion in many countries, including Afghanistan, Algeria, Egypt, Iran, Iraq, Libya, Malaysia, Morocco, Saudi Arabia, and Syria. There are also Muslims in the states of the former Soviet Union, in China, and in Europe as well as on the continents of North and South America. The four countries with the largest Muslim communities are Indonesia, Pakistan, India, and Bangladesh—all in Asia.

Like the Jewish and Christian communities, the Islamic community comprises a large number of groups, among which beliefs

The mosque in Mecca with the black stone of the Kaaba at the center. As the birthplace of the prophet Muhammad, Mecca is one of the three holy cities for Muslims, Medina and Jerusalem being the other two. It was in Mecca, in the early seventh century, that Muhammad began to receive his divine revelation.

differ. There are, however, two overarching divisions within the faith: Most Muslims belong to the Sunni sect and are known as Sunni Muslims; all other Muslims belong to the Shii sects and are known as the Shia. The word "Shiite" is a variation of this term and is commonly used in the Western media. The largest group of Shia are known as the Twelver Shia. They form a majority in Iran and are represented by large communities in Iraq, Kuwait, Lebanon, and India. Several smaller branches of Shii Islam form communities in Yemen, India, and other countries as well.

TWO MISCONCEPTIONS ABOUT ISLAM

Despite its huge following around the world—and growing Muslim communities in the United States—Islam is foreign to most Americans, who are more familiar with Christianity or Judaism. Because most Americans know little or nothing about Islam, they have many misconceptions about Muslim beliefs and rituals. One common misconception is that all Muslims are Arabs. It is true that the Arabian Peninsula was the birthplace of Islam, that in the early years of Islam the majority of Muslims were Arabs, and that the holy text of Islam (the Quran) is written in the Arabic language. However only a century or so after the founding of Islam the religion had spread to parts of southern Europe and east to Central Asia, India, and beyond. As it spread Islam attracted growing numbers of converts among the peoples of these areas. Gradually the Arabs became but one in a variety of peoples that practiced the Muslim religion. As a result most Muslims today are not Arabs. They do not speak Arabic and the great majority live outside of the Middle East

Spellings

Following conventional usage in Arabic, which is increasingly being accepted as conventional use in English, Quran is used instead of Koran, Muslim instead of Moslem, madrasa instead of madrassa, and Hijra instead of Hegira. Conventional English spellings have been retained for Mecca and Medina. When there is reference to Shii Muslims as a group or collectively, the term Shia is used (for example, the Shia). Shii is used as an adjective (for example, Shii law) and as a noun for an individual (for example, he is a Shii). In order to make this book more accessible to the non-specialist, no diacritic markings have been used for foreign words and the terminal *h* has also been dropped (for example, shari'ah is now sharia and sunnah is now sunna).

A Muslim from Zimbabwe, Africa. Islam is widespread particularly in North Africa where Islam is the state religion of Egypt, Mauritania, Morocco, Algeria, Tunisia, Libya, Djibouti, and Somalia.

and North Africa—the two areas where the Arab population of the world is concentrated. Some Arabs are Christian.

PERCEPTIONS OF MUSLIMS

Another misconception is that Muslims are harsh and violent, and especially that they are hostile toward Westerners. Reports of the bombings of the U.S. embassies in Kenya and Tanzania in 1998; of the leveling of New York's Twin Towers on September 11, 2001; of the blasts in Indonesia's Bali in 2002 and 2005; of the destruction of a Catholic church and school, a Presbyterian church, and a Salvation Army Hall in Sangla Hill, Pakistan, in 2005; the torching of thousands of automobiles in the cities of France in the same year; and the unending killing of thousands of coalition soldiers and tens of thousands of native soldiers and civilians in Iraq have filled newspaper pages and television screens throughout the past decade. These acts of Muslim extremists have often been associated with Islam in a way that implies that all Muslims are violent—even that the teachings of Islam advocate violence. In fact the great majority of Muslims are peaceful, as their religion teaches them to be.

HISTORICAL LEGACY

It is not just the recent catastrophes that have led to this portrait of the violent Muslim. The Western image of the hostile Muslim has a long history, beginning with the invasion of Spain in 711 and the spread of the Moors into southern France, where they were repelled by Frankish ruler Charles Martel in 732. Spain itself was finally recaptured only in 1492, when the army of King Ferdinand of Aragon and Queen Isabel of Castile retook Granada. The Crusades, beginning in 1095 and lasting until 1291, pitted Muslims and Christians in battles that left bitter attitudes toward one another. The invasions of Austria and Croatia by the Ottoman Turks in the late 17th century also engendered bad memories of the Turkish Muslims as barbaric and uncivilized. A few scholars and travelers from Europe and later the United States realized that these were ugly stereotypes and tried in vain to paint a more positive picture of Islam and the Muslims. However the image of the barbaric Muslim has survived for centuries and has spread throughout the Western world.

Stereotypes are false generalizations resulting from a lack of understanding. Many have judged Islam and Muslims without making an effort to consider this religious tradition on its own terms and without bothering to become acquainted with its teachings and the ways in which Muslims actually practice their faith. The purpose of this book is to provide a better understanding of Islam so that the reader can begin to go beyond stereotypes.

ISLAM: AN OVERVIEW

Like Judaism and Christianity, Islam is a monotheistic religion—based on the belief in one God. Muslims use the Arabic word for God, *Allah*, to refer to the creator of the world and of all life within it. For Muslims Allah is the lord of the universe.

SUBMISSION TO ALLAH

The word *Islam* is Arabic and means "submission to Allah." According to Islamic belief Allah (the Arabic word for God) has sent a series of revelations to human beings over the course of time. These include the revelations received by Moses and Jesus. The Islamic tradition holds Moses and Jesus, as well as other prophets revered by the Jewish and Christian faiths, in great esteem. However Muslims believe that these revelations, which came to humanity before the revelation of Islam, were corrupted—that human ideas and words were mixed with the divine message and that in their ignorance men and women neglected to follow God's teachings.

GOD'S REVELATION TO MUHAMMAD

Muslims believe that God sent his message to humanity in order to guide those who were faithful to him and to warn the evildoers of his anger. The man whom God chose to receive this new message was Muhammad ibn Abd Allah, a 40-year-old merchant of the Arabic town of Mecca. Sent to Muhammad in the early part of the seventh century, this revelation came to be known as the Quran. To the present day the Quran remains for Muslims the literal Word of God.

Ordered by God to spread the divine revelation, Muhammad slowly won over followers in Mecca and later in the nearby town of Medina. This was the first Islamic community and the seed from which would grow the modern Islamic world.

Muslims believe the Quran is the literal Word of God. As the Quran itself says:

Allah, there is no god but He, the Living, the Self-subsistent.
He has revealed to you the Book with the truth, confirming
that which came before it. He also earlier revealed the Torah
and the Gospel, as a source of guidance for people, and (now)
He has sent down the Salvation.

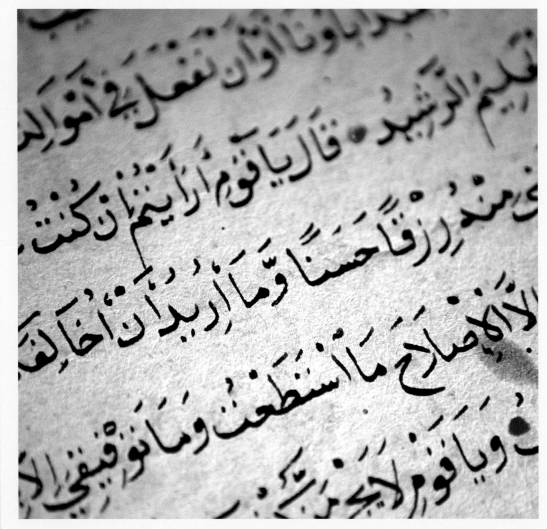

A page from a handwritten Quran.

UMMA—COMMUNITY

Muslims refer to their community as *umma,* an Arabic word meaning "community." For Muslims, *umma* has a special connotation, however, because it occurs many times in the Quran. There the term is used to mean religious community, including the religious communities of Jews and Christians and Muslims.

SHARIA—LAW AND GUIDE

The foundation of the Islamic *umma* is the collection of religious laws and duties known as the sharia. The term is often translated as "holy law," but it is better thought of as the religious path Muslims are expected to follow. For devout Muslims the sharia is a set of regulations whose direct source is God; thus to follow the sharia is to follow and obey God's will.

However the sharia addresses more than matters of prayer and faith in God, which many people think of as strictly religious concerns. It also deals with life in this world—how the community organizes its affairs and how members of the community live their lives. According to the sharia there is no real separation between religion and all other aspects of life. Therefore devout Muslims seek to use the sharia to guide them in every area of their day-to-day lives.

CHAPTER 2

MUHAMMAD AND THE FOUNDING OF ISLAM

Muhammad ibn Abd Allah was born in the trading and pilgrimage city of Mecca, a small but bustling commercial center in the northwestern part of the Arabian Peninsula, around the year 570. He was was a member of the Banu Hashim, one of the town's Arab clans. His father died about the time of Muhammad's birth; his mother died when he was six. The orphan was then cared for by his grandfather, and upon the latter's death two years later, by his uncle Abu Talib. At the time Abu Talib was the head of the Hashim clan.

ARABIA PRIOR TO ISLAM

For most people who lived there Arabia in the late sixth century was a difficult place in which to grow up. Most of the peninsula consisted of desert or arid steppe areas—an environment that demanded a great deal from even the strongest individuals. Only along the southern coastal areas, where higher elevations and sea breezes caused a milder climate, and along the far western mountainous region, was nature less harsh.

At the center of the sacred mosque of Mecca stands the holy Kaaba. In the pre-Islamic period the Kaaba contained a number of idols worshipped by the people of Mecca. Shortly before his death the prophet Muhammad ordered that the idols be destroyed. From that point forward the Kaaba became the sacred sanctuary of Islam.

In the wide stretches of desert life centered on two kinds of communities. On a few oases and in small commercial centers, such as Mecca, people earned a living from agriculture and trading. The majority of the people who lived on the peninsula, however, were nomads who moved each year with their belongings and animals from one grazing area to the next. In both the sedentary and nomadic communities society was organized around clans. These in turn made up larger tribes.

TRIBES AND TRIBAL LEADERS

The tribe was the cornerstone of society in early Arabia. It provided its members with support, protection against enemies, and a sense of identity. Belonging to a powerful tribe that could always protect its members was obviously advantageous.

The tribal leaders, known as shaykhs, usually came from the larger, wealthier clans of each tribe; they made most of the decisions affecting the tribe. Poorer, smaller clans had to abide by the decisions of the larger ones and often resented doing so.

Arab nomads in an area of the Syrian desert. In the seventh century, during the prophet's lifetime, nomadism was a common way of life in many parts of the Middle East including the Arabian Peninsula. Over the past century nomadism has slowly dwindled, in part because many nomadic groups either choose or are forced to settle down and must seek other forms of livelihood.

The nomadic tribes got milk and fresh meat from their flocks and herds as well as the wool and camel hair they needed for clothing, blankets, and tents. Because most tribes were poor and had few possessions apart from their animals, they sometimes raided others for whatever they could carry away. The purpose of the raid, or *ghazwa,* was seldom to kill one's enemies. Rather it was to steal animals, goods, and when possible, women from the opposing tribe. The animals and goods added to the meager wealth of the tribe; the women were either kept or sold as slaves. The raid was also a time for tribes to demonstrate their strength and, for the individual members of the tribe, their courage.

REVENGE AND FEUDS

Although killing the members of opposing tribes was not usually the goal of a raid, it was often unavoidable. Arabia, before the coming of Islam, had no central government; tribes took it upon themselves to avenge the wrongs done to one of their members. As a result vengeance killings were common among nomadic tribes. On occasion these acts of revenge led to costly feuds between tribes. While many decried the human costs of these feuds, there was little anyone could do to prevent them.

Leading a tribe was consequently no easy task. In an environment where threats from nature and from other tribes were constant, only the most practical and courageous could succeed in positions of leadership. Those who displayed such qualities were highly respected by all. Only one other voice in the community was listened to as closely as the shaykh's—that of the poet.

THE INFLUENCE OF THE POET

For the Arabs of this period there was no higher form of expression than poetry. However the poet was more than a valued member of society who sang of the joys and hardships of life. Poets, especially those who showed great eloquence, were believed to be possessed by jinn—the spirits that inhabited the natural world. Thus it was thought that poets had supernatural powers with which they could defeat enemies and often poets were called

Placating the Jinn

In the harsh Arabian environment many people looked to religion for comfort. Although Christianity and Judaism had made inroads into the peninsula by the time of Muhammad's birth, most people practiced forms of religion that were native to their area. They believed, for example, that the jinn (the spirits that inhabited the natural world) could work evil or good, and it was important never to anger them. Consequently in certain areas, such as sites believed to be the burial places of spirits, mounds of stones were erected and offerings, sometimes of food, were left beside these stone markers to please the jinn.

on to use these powers. The early Arabs also revered certain gods and goddesses. Although these divinities varied according to the tribe or area of the peninsula, there seems to have been a common belief in at least one of these gods: Allah, the creator of the universe. Allah was probably considered the supreme god but, unlike the other deities beneath him, he was thought to have little involvement in the daily lives of people.

THE TOWN OF MECCA

In Mecca and the surrounding region, known as the Hijaz, the most popular deities were three goddesses said to be the daughters of Allah. Idols were dedicated to them and often the surrounding area was considered sacred, within which no animal could be killed and in which tribesmen in trouble—for whatever reason—could claim refuge.

THE KAABA—A SACRED SHRINE

At the time of Muhammad's birth Mecca was an important religious center for the tribes of western and central Arabia. Its sanctuary dedicated to the three principal goddesses was located in an area known as the Kaaba, which held idols representing these and other gods and goddesses. The area had been built around a mysterious black stone, perhaps a meteorite, that was venerated by the tribes of the area. Each year local tribesmen visited Mecca to see the Kaaba. The pilgrimage, known as the hajj, included a ceremonial procession around the sacred shrine.

INFLUENCE AND CONTROL IN MECCA

Mecca was therefore not only a commercial but also a religious center. Pilgrims came to worship at the Kaaba and, because it was a sacred shrine around which violence was prohibited, many also came to buy and sell their goods. Those who benefited the most from this activity were the merchant families of Mecca.

By the time of Muhammad's birth the leaders of these families had come to dominate Meccan society because they controlled the flow of goods in and out of the town. They were business-people who recognized that much of the commerce within the town depended upon the pilgrims. To ensure that the pilgrimage ran smoothly these families took control of the sanctuary of the Kaaba. As a result they virtually controlled life in Mecca and the surrounding areas. For these large clans it was a time of prosperity and political strength.

Although these groups certainly benefited from Mecca's prosperity, many other people of the area did not. With the growing commerce had come new sets of values and concerns. Where once the tribe and the health of the community were given priority, now materialism and a new concern with individual wealth and power undermined traditional values. Increasingly the larger clans dominated the smaller, poorer ones, denying them a share in the town's growing wealth. As values changed and the gap between rich and poor widened, resentment among the less fortunate began to intensify.

A tile from Istanbul painted with a drawing of the Kaaba. When Muslims visit the Kaaba, they try to come close enough to kiss the black stone which is shown in the center of this tile.

SPIRITUAL QUESTIONS

It was an uneasy world into which Muhammad was born. The shift from communal values to a more individualistic way of life caused many to ask difficult questions about the world around them. These questions were less about money and power and more about the meaning of the world and individual destiny. Traditional practices and beliefs no longer provided the answers these people were seeking. For many it was a time of spiritual uneasiness.

The lights from a minaret shine out as night falls. In Muslim countries the call for Muslims to come to prayer is made five times a day from the top of the minaret.

Some may have converted to Christianity or to Judaism, which had spread to the Arabian Peninsula. Jewish tribes had lived in the town of Yathrib—a prosperous agricultural center not far from Mecca—for generations and were a well-established part of the community. Although no Christian tribes inhabited Arabia at the time, there were numerous Christian Arabs in areas north of the peninsula. These groups, which comprised various Christian sects, were ruled by the Byzantine Empire, the capital of which was Constantinople (known today as Istanbul, the largest city in Turkey). The merchants of Mecca no doubt traded with these Christians regularly.

MUHAMMAD'S EARLY LIFE

In Mecca the powerful merchant clans remained in control of religious life and presumably were careful not to allow across the borders new practices and beliefs such as Christianity or Judaism, both of which were being practiced in the area at this time. Meccans who did not travel therefore sought new beliefs and religious guidance within Mecca itself. The orphan Muhammad was soon to fulfill this need.

EXPERIENCING THE OUTSIDE WORLD

Little is known about Muhammad's early life. His uncle Abu Talib provided him with clothing and a home but never taught him to read or write. Later in his life Muhammad depended on his followers to write down the words of the revelation in order to preserve them. It is believed that in his teens Muhammad worked as a camel driver, accompanying his uncle and other merchants on their travels into southern Syria and on the peninsula itself. In this way Muhammad gained exposure to places outside of Mecca and grew familiar with their different customs. For the most part the Meccans traded with other Arab tribes and the settled Arabic-speaking population of Syria. Because these included Christian communities Muhammad came into contact with this monotheistic tradition. How much he actually learned about Christian beliefs remains uncertain.

MARRIAGE INTO THE MERCHANT CLASS

In the year 595 Muhammad's life took a dramatic turn. For a time he had been working for an older merchant—a wealthy woman named Khadija. He had shown himself to be intelligent and responsible, impressing her so much that she proposed marriage. He accepted and thus became a successful member of the Meccan merchant class.

During the next 15 years Muhammad enjoyed a life of prosperity. As a merchant he continued to travel to other areas of the peninsula and farther north, encountering the ideas and practices of Jewish and Christian communities. Again, it is hard to tell what he learned about these beliefs.

Unlike other merchants Muhammad found only passing satisfaction with the comforts such a life provided. He seems to have been aware of the decline in traditional values within Meccan society and of the unhappiness felt by many in the area. Having known poverty as a young boy, Muhammad was sensitive to the grievances of the less fortunate. He began to question the direction that both his life and that of his community was taking.

THE COMING OF REVELATION

By the age of 40 Muhammad had begun to spend time alone, meditating on the questions that troubled him. On occasion he would spend nights in a small cave near Mecca. It was common for men to go on retreat, so few thought his behavior odd. During one such night Muhammad experienced what he thought were strange visions. As Muslims are taught, the angel Gabriel appeared before him in human form. Seizing hold of Muhammad, the angel ordered him to recite a short set of words. When he did so the angel released him.

Overwhelmed by his visions and the message he received, at first Muhammad told only Khadija and a few close followers. Slowly he began to preach more openly to the Meccan community. As the biographers of Muhammad tell us, Muhammad continued to receive revelations for the next 20 years, and until the end of his life he passed them on to his followers. This is why Muslims call Muhammad the Messenger of God.

At first Muhammad's message was a simple one: He declared that there was only one god, Allah, and that there was nothing like him. Like the prophets before him Muhammad also preached of the power of God and the certainty that the day of judgment was to come.

At first Muhammad's preaching was ignored by the leaders of Mecca. They had heard similar ideas from Jews and Christians, so they assumed that Muhammad was only repeating those ideas. Before long, however, the Meccans began to realize the meaning of Muhammad's teach-

THE MESSENGER OF GOD

After a vision of the angel Gabriel first appeared while he was spending the night in a small cave near Mecca, Muhammad was convinced that either he was losing his mind or spirits had possessed him, and he fled from the cave. Partly down the hill he heard a voice behind him say, "Oh, Muhammad, you are the Messenger of God, and I am Gabriel."

Confused and terrified, Muhammad was convinced his sanity had left him. Only as the experiences continued—and with the encouragement of his wife, Khadija, who was sure the words came from God—did Muhammad come to believe that the words he was asked to recite were revelations from God and that God now expected him to serve as his divine messenger.

ings. For instance Muhammad called on people to worship only Allah and to reject the cult of the goddesses. He stressed that to worship any other deity—whether goddess, idol, or jinn—was to violate the absolute oneness of God.

These teachings challenged the entire system upon which Meccan leaders had established their power and wealth. Realizing that if Muhammad succeeded in convincing people of the truth of his message, that structure would collapse, they were determined to see that Muhammad failed.

THE OPPOSITION TO MUHAMMAD

As the top Meccan families turned against Muhammad, using threats and insults as well as physical violence, Muhammad realized that he and his followers must leave Mecca. In the year 619 they moved to Taaif, a nearby town, for refuge, but the main tribe of Taaif, the Banu Thaqif, refused to let them remain and they were obliged to make their way back to Mecca.

This was only one in a series of setbacks for Muhammad in 619. Two of his most loyal supporters had died earlier that year: his beloved wife, Khadija, and his uncle Abu Talib. With the death of Abu Talib, who had protected the Muslims, Muhammad lost an important friend.

THE JOURNEY TO HEAVEN

However the year 619 was marked not only by sadness; it was also the year in which, according to the Islamic tradition, Muhammad experienced one of the most remarkable events of his life. Asleep one night near the Kaaba, Muhammad was awakened by the angel Gabriel. With Gabriel as his guide Muhammad journeyed to Jerusalem and then, from a prominent rock, to heaven. There he is said to have met with the great prophets Abraham, Jesus, Moses, and others. At the climax

The Prophet of God

It took Muhammad several years to overcome his initial doubts and to realize the importance of his task. However by 613 he was convinced that he was meant to follow in the footsteps of the prophets before him—Abraham, Moses, and Jesus, among others—and to bring God's word to humanity. As a result Muhammad assumed the title Prophet of God and began to preach openly in the streets.

of his journey Muhammad is believed to have stood before God. For Muslims this miraculous journey is further evidence of Muhammad's profound spiritual nature.

AN OUTSIDER TO RESTORE PEACE

Muhammad still faced the hostility of the Meccans. It became essential that he find a place outside Mecca that would welcome him and his followers. The solution came in the year 620. Among the pilgrims who visited Mecca that year was a group of men from the northern town of Yathrib (also known as Medina). The men had heard of Muhammad and were impressed with his teachings. In their first meeting with him they told him of the problems facing their town. Rival tribes had taken up arms in a bloody feud and chaos threatened the town. Having failed to find a solution, the men had come seeking an outsider who could restore peace.

Over the next two years the men returned to Mecca with others from Medina, and a group of them converted to Islam. Encouraged by this new support Muhammad urged his Meccan followers to make their way to Medina, where they could begin a new life as Muslims. Gradually they left Mecca and traveled north to what would become their home for roughly the next decade.

The Hijra

Muhammad's journey from Mecca to Medina is one of the key events of Muhammad's life. It signaled not only his escape to safety but, far more important, the establishment of the Islamic community. The journey is known to Muslims as the Hijra, and the event came to be recognized as marking the beginning of the Islamic calendar.

MUHAMMAD'S ESCAPE FROM MECCA

When Muhammad received word that a group of Meccans were planning to kill him, he arranged to leave Mecca that very night. In late September 622 Muhammad and his closest adviser, Abu Bakr, made their way to a cave outside the town. There they hid from the assassins for three days.

The golden dome of the Dome of the Rock, a shrine in Jerusalem. For Muslims this marks the site where Muhammad ascended on a night journey to heaven to meet the great prophets and to stand before God.

According to legend the mouth of the cave was covered by the web of a spider moments before the Meccans rode by. One of the assassins glanced down from his horse, saw the delicate web covering the entrance, and remarked that surely no one could be inside the cave.

With the way clear Muhammad and Abu Bakr traveled to Medina, where they were greeted joyfully by the waiting Muslims and their Medinan supporters.

MUHAMMAD: POLITICS AND PROPHETHOOD

The community of Muslims that welcomed Muhammad to Medina was made up of both Meccans and Medinans. Muhammad knew that he had to avoid showing favoritism to either group. In one of his first decisions as leader of this community, he demonstrated his political skills. Faced with offers from both groups to make his home with them, he wisely avoided making the decision. He simply let his camel roam free and at the spot where the animal came to rest, Muhammad established his home. Huts were erected for Muhammad and the two women he had married since the death of Khadija in 619. Beside these a large space was cleared and a rough structure built. This was the first mosque, or place of worship for followers of Islam, built in Medina. Muhammad was now set to continue his divinely appointed task.

CHALLENGES FOR THE MUSLIM COMMUNITY

Muhammad's responsibilities in Medina were daunting. Not only did he continue receiving revelations from God and teaching his followers, but he was now also the leader of the young Muslim community. He faced a host of problems: He had to find a solution to the feuds that were dividing the town, he had to find work and shelter for the Meccans who had come to Medina with him, he had to counter opposition to the teachings of Islam within Medina, and he still faced the challenge of the Meccan merchant clans that were determined to see him and his community destroyed.

In solving the problems between the Medinans Muhammad convinced the feuding clans that they should join the community of Muslims. He worked out a series of agreements that forged strong links between the Meccans and those Medinans who accepted his teachings. He faced, however, mounting distrust from one group in Medina—the Jewish tribes.

CONFLICT WITH THE JEWISH TRIBES

Three tribes made up the Jewish population of Medina. At first they had welcomed Muhammad because of the peace he promised to bring. Soon however they began to have second thoughts about his leadership and his teachings. Initially Muhammad considered incorporating certain Jewish practices into the rituals of Islam, and for a time Muslims and Jews prayed together in the direction of Jerusalem. Then in the year 624 Muhammad received inspiration from God to instruct his followers to pray in the direction of Mecca. This caused a break with the Jewish tribes. From that point forward relations between the Jews of Medina and the Muslim community worsened and ended finally in violence. Two of the Jewish tribes were driven from Medina while the male members of the third tribe suffered execution at the hands of the Muslims.

FARMING AND RAIDING

Muhammad turned his attention to the problem of providing for those of his followers who had come with him from Mecca. Medina was an agricultural town, but the Meccan Muslims lacked experience in farming. Instead of having them learn to farm Muhammad decided to have them engage in a more familiar activity—raiding. Arming his male followers Muhammad sent them against the trade caravans that crossed the peninsula. A series of raids were carried out successfully and in this way the Muslim community was able to provide for its needs.

THE CLASH OF ARMS

The Meccans were outraged. They depended on the caravan trade for their livelihood and viewed these attacks as an attempt by Muhammad to undermine their power. Their opportunity to respond to the Muslims came in the year 624. A large caravan was reported to be on its way to Mecca from the north. Expecting the Muslims to launch a raid, the Meccans sent a strong force to escort the caravan into the area.

Muhammad had indeed sent a group of Muslim raiders against the caravan. At a place named Badr the two small forces clashed. Although the Muslims were outnumbered 3 to 1 they fought bravely and finally routed the Meccan fighters. This victory was seen by the Muslims as proof of divine guidance and evidence that they were indeed chosen by God for a special purpose.

DEFEAT AND A TEST OF FAITH

The following year the Meccan leadership set out to avenge the loss at Badr. Organizing a huge force, they set out against Muhammad and his people. The two armies met near the mountain of Uhud and this time the Muslims met with defeat, losing both dead and wounded to the Meccans. This came as a blow to

A night scene at the Prophet's Mosque in Medina. In the year 622 Prophet Muhammad left Mecca to escape the hostility of the Meccans and made his way to Medina. This event is known as the Hijra. In Medina the prophet established the first Muslim community.

the Muslims, some of whom questioned whether God was really behind Muhammad and his community. The debate was settled when a revelation came to Muhammad in which the defeat was represented as a test for the true believer. Those who held firmly to their beliefs would find reward from God.

CONFLICTS WITH MECCANS AND THE JEWISH TRIBES

Despite their victory the Meccans returned to Mecca, giving the Muslims a chance to regroup. The following year the Muslims faced perhaps their greatest challenge from Mecca. In an effort to crush the Muslim community the Meccans organized a huge force and marched on Medina. Following the advice of one of his followers Muhammad had a long trench dug in front of Medina. The trench prevented the Meccans from riding up to the town. After a time the Meccan forces grew restless, many of the nomads in the army left, and the campaign was called off. Although little fighting had taken place the Muslims viewed the event as a victory—and further proof that God was on their side.

Following this battle Muhammad turned against the last of the Jewish tribes. The tribe had negotiated with the Meccans and so was accused by the Muslims of treachery. After surrendering to Muhammad's forces the men of the tribe were put to the sword, and the women and children were sold into slavery. This brought to an end all opposition to Muhammad within Medina. Muhammad now resumed his efforts to defeat his sworn enemies—the leaders of Mecca.

In the hope of settling matters without further bloodshed Muhammad announced that he and a group of Muslims would go to Mecca to perform the traditional ceremonies at the Kaaba. When they reached Mecca, however, they were met by an armed force. Muhammad insisted his intentions were peaceful but the Meccan forces would not budge. After heated negotiations the Muslims agreed to leave and not return until the following year, when they would enter the city to perform the ceremonies. While many Muslims were disappointed with the decision not to attack Mecca, Muhammad told them that the agreement represented recognition from the Meccans of Muhammad's leadership and of the strength of the Muslim community—and thus it was a victory for them and for Islam.

VICTORY OVER OPPOSING TRIBES AND THE SURRENDER OF MECCA

Having set aside the issue of the Meccans for the moment Muhammad sought to subdue those tribes of the region that had

The *mihrab* in the Sultan Hassan mosque in Cairo, Egypt. The *mihrab*, a small niche located in all mosques, indicates the proper direction of prayer. Muslims must pray in the direction of Mecca, the site of the holy Kaaba.

supported his enemies. He marched on the town of Khaybar, which his forces took after a prolonged siege. Then the Muslims moved steadily against other tribes that had allied with their enemies. One by one they defeated these tribes and made them swear allegiance to Islam. With these victories Muhammad's hold over the peninsula was secure.

The following year the Meccans opened their town to the Muslims, who peacefully carried out the ceremonies under the leadership of Muhammad. The next year, however, tensions reemerged and Muhammad decided to use force against the Meccans. With his army Muhammad marched on Mecca ready for battle. As he approached the city, however, he was met by the head of the Meccans, Abu Sufyan, who had decided that Mecca could no longer resist the Muslims. Abu Sufyan surrendered the town and the sacred sanctuary to Muhammad.

VICTORY AND THE FINAL PILGRIMAGE

The year was 630 and Muhammad stayed for only a short time in Mecca—long enough to establish Muslim control over the town and to win the support of the Meccan population. For the next two years Muhammad expanded his influence throughout the Arabian Peninsula. He sent envoys to distant tribes, calling on them to convert to Islam. Many of the tribes did so with little protest, whereas others were convinced only with the use of force. Before long Muhammad controlled most of the peninsula.

THE LAST GREAT SERMON

In the year 632 Muhammad again set out for Mecca to perform the annual pilgrimage to the Kaaba. In previous years

KAABA, THE CENTRAL SANCTUARY

Entering the town of Mecca after its surrender Muhammad proceeded directly to the Kaaba, a sanctuary dedicated to the three principal goddesses that held idols representing these and other gods and goddesses. Placing his hand upon the black stone (a mysterious stone, perhaps a meteorite, which the Kaaba had been built around) Muhammad shouted in a clear voice, *"Allahu Akbar"* (God is most great). With this Muhammad was affirming the most basic of Islamic beliefs—the supreme oneness of God. He then ordered that the idols of the Kaaba be destroyed. This brought an end to the cult of the goddesses and the use of the Kaaba as a shrine of this cult. The Kaaba, from that moment on, was claimed by the Muslims as the central sanctuary of the Islamic religion, a status it retains to the present day.

Muhammad had permitted both Muslims and non-Muslims to carry out the pilgrimage. This year, however, he ruled that now only Muslims could worship at the Kaaba. From that time forward the rituals and the sacred sanctuary were to be dedicated solely to the worship of Allah.

On the 10th day of the pilgrimage, after the required rituals, Muhammad spoke to the Muslims in his last great sermon. He spoke to them of their obligations as members of the community of Muslims and he urged them to treat each other well and thus maintain the unity of Islam.

THE FAREWELL PILGRIMAGE

With the pilgrimage complete, Muhammad left for Medina. Known as the Farewell Pilgrimage, this was to be the last time Muhammad would see Mecca and the Kaaba. Not long after his return to Medina Muhammad fell ill, and late on the 12th day of Rabi I, the third month of the Islamic calendar, he died.

THE FINAL REVELATION

Muhammad ended his last sermon with this reminder: "I have left amongst you that which, if you hold fast to it, shall preserve you from all error, a clear indication, the Book of God, and the word of His Prophet. O, people, hear my words and understand."

He then recited to them the final revelation, one it is believed he had received from God only a short time earlier:

*Today the unbelievers have despaired of
  your religion;
therefore fear them not, but
  fear you Me.
Today I have perfected your religion
  for you,
and I have completed My blessing
  upon you,
and I have approved Islam for
  your religion.*

—Quran 5.3

The Islamic community now faced a troubling question: Who was to lead the community now that Muhammad was gone? In bringing the Quran to humankind, he had fulfilled his tasks as the messenger of God. However he had also founded a community that had come to depend upon his leadership and teachings. After Muhammad's death it was up to the community to find a successor.

CHAPTER 3

THE SPREAD OF ISLAM

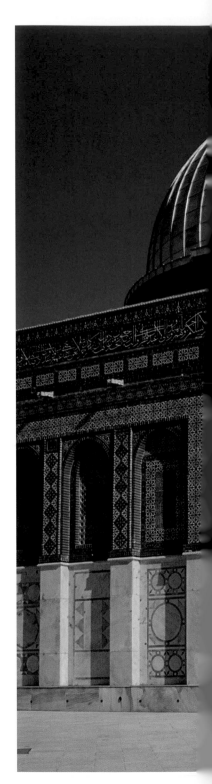

Muhammad had not left instructions on how to choose a successor. The Muslims had to resolve this problem as best they could.

On the evening of Muhammad's death a group of Muslims debated the issue. Finally they selected Abu Bakr as their new leader. He had been one of the first Meccans to convert to Islam and had consistently shown his loyalty to Muhammad. The decision was approved by the community and Abu Bakr was given the title of caliph, or successor, which meant that he took over Muhammad's role as the political leader of the Islamic community. The state that he and those who ruled after him would run would be called the caliphate.

THE FIRST THREE CALIPHS AND THE EARLY CONQUESTS

Under the leadership of Abu Bakr an important step was taken by the Islamic community: the final conquest of the Arabian Peninsula. During Muhammad's lifetime most of the Arab tribes in

A close-up of the Dome of the Rock in Jerusalem. Muslims believe that it was from this site that Muhammad journeyed to heaven. The building was erected in the late seventh century by an Umayyad caliph. In the 16th century the exterior walls were redecorated by the Ottomans, then rulers of a large Islamic empire with its capital in Istanbul.

Arabia had agreed to accept the teachings of Islam. Following his death, however, many broke away. Abu Bakr sent forces to bring these tribes back under the rule of Islam. Within a short time the entire peninsula fell under Muslim control.

The decision to send forces beyond the limits of the Arabian Peninsula had been made earlier by Muhammad. Since he died before carrying out these plans, it was up to Abu Bakr and his successors to do so.

BYZANTINES AND SASSANIANS

The Middle East was then controlled by two rival empires. In the areas of what is today called Syria, Egypt, and Turkey, the Byzantine Empire held sway. Further to the east, in Iraq and Iran, was the empire of the Sassanians. For decades conflict between the two empires had weakened them both politically and economically. Neither empire was prepared to meet the unexpected threat from the Arabian Peninsula to the south.

Although Abu Bakr organized the first attacks against Syria and Iraq, he died shortly after the fighting began in 634. The position of caliph then passed to Umar ibn al-Khattab. Umar, who would rule over the Muslims for about a decade, proved to be an excellent choice. Under his leadership Muslims ran successful campaigns against the Byzantine and Sassanian empires.

UTHMAN, THE THIRD CALIPH

With Umar's death in 644 a new caliph was chosen for the growing empire. He was Uthman ibn Affan, a merchant from the Umayyad family. This family had been opposed to Muhammad when he began his preaching in Mecca and after his move

ISLAM UNDER CALIPH UMAR

Skilled in both politics and military strategy, Umar is considered one of the greatest figures of early Islamic history because under his leadership the Islamic empire flourished and spread. He sent his armies deep into Syria, where they defeated the forces of the Byzantine Empire (395–1453). They captured the cities of Damascus and Jerusalem and then moved against Egypt, where once again Byzantine forces were defeated and sent into full retreat north.

Meanwhile Muslim armies battled the Persian Sassanid dynasty (ca. 224–651) throughout Iraq and Iran. In several battles the Muslims inflicted heavy losses on the Persian troops. Although Umar would not live to see the final collapse of the Sassanid Empire, by the end of his life all of Iraq and a large area of Iran had fallen into Muslim hands.

to Medina. Although the family finally converted to Islam there were still bad feelings between the Umayyads and other groups within the Islamic community. During Uthman's caliphate these feelings deepened until many Muslims began to oppose Uthman.

Under Uthman Muslim forces continued to conquer new areas: From Egypt they pushed west into North Africa, and in Iran they continued to defeat the Sassanians. Soon, however, the Muslims were forced to turn their attention to the increasing tension between Uthman and various groups within the community

MUSLIM AGAINST MUSLIM

Tensions finally exploded in the year 656 with the assassination of Uthman. Although a new caliph was quickly chosen Uthman's murder sent shock waves throughout the community and led to civil war. For the first time Muslims were armed against each other. The man chosen to succeed Uthman was Ali ibn Abi Talib, the son-in-law and cousin of Muhammad and one of his earliest converts. Though highly respected for his close relationship with Muhammad and for his service to Islam, Ali soon found himself in serious trouble.

MUSLIM CONFLICT: ALI AND MUAWIYAH

Uthman's family, the Umayyads, was now led by Muawiyah, who was then the Muslim governor of Syria. He was critical of Ali for not having done enough to punish Uthman's killers. When Ali tried to make Muawiyah step down as governor, Muawiyah refused; Ali felt obliged to send an army against him. At first Ali's troops did well against the Syrian forces but Muawiyah was able to convince Ali to open negotiations. Ali agreed and the fighting was stopped. It was a decision that Ali was soon to regret.

CALIPHS IN THE FIRST PERIOD OF ISLAMIC HISTORY

Death of the prophet Muhammad: **632**
First caliph:
    Abu Bakr: **632–634**
Second caliph:
    Umar ibn al-Khattab: **634–644**
Third caliph:
    Uthman ibn Affan: **644–656**
Fourth caliph:
    Ali ibn Abi Talib: **656–661**

After the death of Ali ibn Abi Talib in 661 Muawiyah took the title of fifth caliph and moved the capital of the empire from Medina to Damascus.

The core of Ali's army was made up of his closest followers. When Ali opened talks with Muawiyah and the Syrian forces a group of these followers broke with him, saying that he did not have the right to halt the fighting. Fiercely devout Muslims, they argued that only God had the power to make such a decision. In their view the only person with the right to rule the community was the successor to Muhammad, who was now Ali; anyone who challenged the ruler was standing against the community and, worse, against the will of God. They argued that because Ali had not defended the community by defeating Muawiyah he had gone against God and therefore was no longer worthy of being ruler.

DEATH OF ALI—THE FOURTH CALIPH

This group of dissidents, known as the Kharijites, now took up arms against the community. Ali, as ruler, had little choice but to send troops against his former followers. In several clashes he was able to subdue the Kharijites. He was not able to crush the movement completely, however, and in 662 a Kharijite stabbed Ali to death.

Civil strife had created deep divisions within the Islamic community and it was not clear who would rule. Into this vacuum stepped Muawiyah, who was still governor of Syria and head of a powerful army. Claiming the title of caliph for himself, Muawiyah moved the capital of the empire from Medina to Damascus. Although many opposed this decision no other group could challenge Muawiyah.

THE UMAYYADS AND THE SHIA

The move to Damascus brought an end to the first period of Islamic history. What had once been a small community of Muslims centered around Muhammad had become a powerful empire in control of a large part of the Middle East and North Africa. A new dynasty, the Umayyads, was now in control of the caliphate and it faced all the problems that come with trying to run a huge empire.

OPPONENTS OF THE UMAYYADS

Among these problems was the opposition of the Kharijites. Although they had been defeated by Ali the Kharijites continued to attract followers with their radical message that the Umayyads had seized power against the will of God. Branding these rulers as illegitimate, they called for Muslims to rise up against the dynasty. In response the Umayyads sent a series of forces against the Kharijites but with mixed results. Although they defeated the radicals in battle, they could not squash the spread and influence of Kharijite ideas.

The Umayyads also faced opposition from the followers of Ali ibn Abi Talib and his family. As an early convert to Islam Ali had attracted an intensely loyal group of followers known as the Shiat Ali, or the Followers of Ali. These Shiis, as they came to be known, fought with Ali against Muawiyah and the Umayyads. Although Ali's assassination shook them deeply they remained loyal to both his name and his family.

The courtyard of the Umayyad mosque in Damascus, originally the cathedral of the city. Besides being a place of prayer the mosque was also a focus for the community, with areas for study, debate, administration, and a place of refuge for the sick and the homeless.

SHIA AND THE FAMILY OF MUHAMMAD

The Shia believed that when Muhammad died he had intended for Ali to succeed him as leader of the community. They argued that Muhammad had given a sermon in which he said that after he was gone the Muslims should follow Ali. For this reason, when Abu Bakr, Umar, and Uthman were chosen as the next caliphs, the Shia protested, saying that only Ali and his family had the right to lead the community after Muhammad. The Shia would remain from this time forward a minority Islamic sect—often persecuted by the majority of Muslims, who belonged to the Sunni branch of Islam and found the Shia's beliefs unacceptable.

After Ali's death the Shia turned their attention to Ali's son, Hasan. At the time Hasan was a religious scholar in the town of Medina, and he stayed clear of politics, to the disappointment of the Shia, until his death in 669. The loyalties of the Shia then shifted to his brother, Husayn. Although cautious, Husayn was proud of his family's name. When the Shia urged him to claim his right to the caliphate in the year 680, Husayn agreed to try. Only a short time before, news had come of the death of Muawiyah. Muawiyah's son Yazid had taken over, but the Shia felt that the time was ripe for revolt. Their center of activity was the city of Kufah. They sent messengers to Husayn in Medina, urging him to come to Kufah to lead them against the hated Umayyads.

HUSAYN'S DEFEAT AND DEATH

Husayn decided to take his chances. He set out for Kufah with his family and a small band of followers. The Umayyad caliph, Yazid, hearing news of Husayn's march, immediately sent troops to prevent the group from reaching Kufah. Near the town of Karbala tragedy struck. Husayn and his small group were attacked by the Umayyad troops. One by one Husayn's followers fell, followed finally by Husayn himself. It is said that the soldiers hesitated before dealing the final blow to the grandson of the prophet.

Husayn is said then to have been beheaded by one of the soldiers. His head was sent to the caliph Yazid in Damascus. Yazid gloated over the head and made crude remarks about Husayn and the rest of Ali's family. For his role in Husayn's death, Yazid would never be forgiven by the Shia.

The killing of Husayn did not bring an end to the activities of the Shia, many of whom began looking to other members of Ali's family to lead them. During the next few decades these men would lead revolts against the Umayyads but with no success. For the Umayyads the Shia remained a thorny problem.

THE UMAYYADS AND NEW CONQUESTS

Although the Umayyads were eventually overthrown the Shia continued to see them as the symbol of unjust government. Even today when the Shia criticize modern political leaders, they often compare them to the Umayyads of the seventh century.

The Umayyad dynasty lasted for roughly 100 years during which the Islamic Empire grew in both size and power. Umayyad forces extended the rule of Islam west across North Africa to the Atlantic coast. Turning north the Muslim armies crossed the Straits of Gibraltar and invaded Spain. They moved swiftly across Spain and into southern France. Only in the year 732 were they finally halted by a Frankish army under the command of Charles Martel. Despite this defeat Spain remained in Muslim hands. For the next 750 years Spain would be a dynamic Islamic land.

The Umayyad armies continued to drive eastward. The remaining areas of Iran fell to the Muslims, as did Afghanistan and the area now called Pakistan. With these new possessions the empire reached new levels of power. Much of the wealth of the Umayyad caliphate came from the taxes that the caliphs imposed on the peoples conquered over the years.

For all their authority the Umayyads still faced serious political problems. The Kharijites and the Shia were still active, and both groups spread propaganda against the Umayyads. On occasion one or the other of the two movements would organize a bloody revolt. Nor were these the only groups opposed to the Umayyads; many other Muslims were angry with the ruling dynasty. One common complaint was that wealth and privileges were not fairly distributed by the Umayyads and their supporters.

These feelings of frustration helped fuel a revolutionary movement that had secretly been forming in the eastern province of Khurasan, which is today part of Central Asia. By the year 750 the Umayyad family was on the defensive, and much of the empire had fallen into the hands of the revolutionaries, who at that point selected a new caliph for the empire: Abu al-Abbas. He was a member of the Abbasid family and ruled only for a short time before his brother, al-Mansur, came to power. Al-Mansur ruled for many years.

THE ABBASID CALIPHATE

The Abbasids ruled from 750 to 1258. In the first 200 years of their rule they reached dizzying heights of power and wealth. Their empire stretched from Morocco to India and the Abbasid caliphs earned the respect of the entire world. Their wealth came from many different sources. With their army and navy the caliphs controlled the trade routes that crisscrossed the empire. Their empire produced vast amounts of agricultural products and took in revenue through taxation, allowing the early Abbasids to live comfortably in great splendor.

To run their empire the Abbasids developed a large bureaucratic government centered in Baghdad. Soon this new capital became a major urban center—the hub of political and economic activity for the whole empire. To defend themselves and the empire they established a powerful standing army based in garrisons throughout the Islamic lands. An impressive intelligence network backed the army with informants who worked in every corner of the empire. The most important army was kept in Baghdad, where it could defend the ruling family and the state.

Among the accomplishments of this period was the development of the Islam-

Arabian Nights

Under the early Abbasid caliphs the Islamic community experienced a period of cultural brilliance. In Baghdad and other cities the caliphs used their influence to encourage poets, writers, and musicians. As a result many great works were created in this period, including the famous *Arabian Nights* (also known as *One Thousand and One Nights*), a collection of Arabic popular narrative tales that encompasses adventure, war, trickery, love, animal fables, travel stories, folktales, and historical anecdotes.

ic legal system. The basis of this new code was, of course, the Quran and the teachings of Muhammad. Using these two sources as their guide the scholars worked out a set of laws and regulations that came to be known as the sharia. As they saw it this was to be the foundation of Islamic society. To enforce these laws and regulations the scholars also worked with the government to establish an Islamic court system. At the head of this new system were the chief judges, the qadis.

THE COLLAPSE OF THE EMPIRE

By the middle of the 10th century the Islamic Empire had given birth to a new and great civilization. The Arabic language and the religion of Islam had taken root throughout the Middle East, North Africa, Spain, and Central Asia. In law, religion, education, art, science, and commerce the Islamic community was living through a golden age. By comparison, Europe was in the midst of the "Dark Ages."

Ornate tilework in a mosque in Isfahan, Iran. Many mosques feature calligraphy and geometric and floral motifs since representations of God and human beings are not permitted.

DIVISIONS AND DEFEAT

Although the cultural achievements during the Abbasid rule would live on, the 10th century brought new political problems that the caliphs proved unable to solve. Preserving the unity of the empire was especially difficult. For more than a century, through diplomacy and the strength of the army, the Abbasid caliphs had controlled the empire. By the ninth century this control began to slip. In North Africa and other regions local leaders began to go their own way. Often they continued to recognize the leadership of the caliph while establishing their own rule over a particular region.

The Abbasids commissioned architects and builders to construct palaces and magnificent homes in the capital and other regions. For a short period the capital was moved to the city of Samarra, like Baghdad on the Tigris River, where the ruins of the many palaces built by this dynasty are still visible.

The Abbasids also provided a great deal of support to the scholarly community. In Baghdad and other cities brilliant work was carried out in intellectual centers. Working with Jewish and Christian scholars, Muslim thinkers set out to translate and study the works of other great cultures, including Greece and India. Many works of mathematics, medicine, theology, and philosophy were translated into the Arabic language. Using these works the Muslims created their own bodies of original ideas, which they laid out in the many books written during this period.

By the middle of the 10th century the caliphs were forced to recognize the end of their power. In 945 a strong army led by a Persian family named the Buwayhids swept into Iraq and captured Baghdad. Although they allowed the caliph to retain his official title, they ran the empire.

Another development further divided the Islamic world in the late 10th century. Earlier in the century a group of Shiis had succeeded in establishing a small state in North Africa. From this center of power they launched attacks to the west, against Egypt. In 969 these leaders, called the Fatimid dynasty, conquered Egypt and established a new city, Cairo, which became their capital. This dynasty would rule Egypt for 200 years, during which it would be in almost constant conflict with the Sunni regions, which were still under the nominal rule of the Abbasid caliphs.

Fatimid rule came to an end in 1171 when Cairo was overrun by the army of Salah al-Din al-Ayyubi, known in the West as Saladin. His victory brought an end to Shii rule in Egypt and was warmly welcomed by the inhabitants of Egypt. Most of them had never accepted Shii beliefs, preferring to remain Sunnis or Christians. While happy to receive their praises, Salah al-Din had to turn his energies to Jerusalem, then under the rule of the Christian Crusade forces.

THE CRUSADES

The Crusades were a series of campaigns launched over four centuries, beginning with an attack on Jerusalem at the end of the 11th century, to return it to Christian rule. Initially the Christian armies succeeded in achieving their goal—the conquest of Jerusalem. This victory in 1099 was followed by the establishment of small kingdoms along the Mediterranean coast.

The fall of Jerusalem came as a shock to many Muslims. To them Jerusalem was of great symbolic importance. It was, according to Islamic belief, from Jerusalem that Muhammad had traveled on his miraculous journey to heaven. The Umayyad caliphs

THE RULE OF THE FATIMIDS

At the height of their power the Fatimids (969–1171) ruled over a large area that included Egypt, large parts of Syria, Persia, the Arabian Peninsula, and North Africa. As a result it became a powerful state. Under the Fatimids Egypt experienced a period of great cultural achievement and Cairo became a large, bustling city. The Fatimids built a series of mosques and palaces throughout Cairo, many of which can still be seen today. Among their accomplishments was the creation of the al-Azhar mosque complex—a religious and educational center that would survive the fall of the Fatimid dynasty in the 12th century. Today it is a major university, attracting students from all over the Islamic world. Originally a center of Shii education, it is now a center of Sunni thought.

View from the Citadel of Old Cairo with the al-Azhar mosque and university in the foreground.

had built a famous mosque, the Dome of the Rock, on the site believed to be the place from which Muhammad started on this journey. Many Muslims grew determined to see the city back in Muslim hands.

It fell to Salah al-Din to organize an army to carry out the task. After taking Egypt he had gone on to conquer Syria and Mesopotamia, thus establishing a unified state. From this position of strength he sent his army against the Crusaders in 1187. After defeating the Christian army his troops reestablished Islamic rule over Jerusalem.

Meanwhile in Baghdad the Abbasid caliphs continued as mere figureheads. The empire over which the dynasty had once ruled was now broken into many small parts. Most of these states were controlled by military men who had little interest in religious matters. Deep political and religious differences divided the Islamic community.

MONGOL CONQUEST OF BAGHDAD

During the early part of the 13th century Mongol armies had been sweeping across the vast lands of China and Russia, moving west into Central Asia. By the 1250s the Mongols, under their leader Hulagu, moved swiftly through Persia and to the gates of Baghdad. There they demanded complete surrender from the last Abbasid caliph, al-Mustasim. With few political and no military forces at his disposal, the caliph had little choice but to agree. Baghdad was overrun by the Mongol troops. The caliph and his family were later taken to a small village and executed, bringing a sad end to the once powerful Abbasid caliphate.

THREE NEW MUSLIM EMPIRES

Never again would one dynasty rule over the whole of the Islamic world. The death of the last Abbasid caliph closed a long and often glorious chapter in the history of Islam. In the heyday of the caliphate the power and cultural achievements of the Islamic world were renowned. The political unity of the empire that had made much of this possible was now at an end. What had not ended, however, were the deep spiritual and cultural links between the many regions of the Islamic world.

Even with the achievements of the Abbasid caliphate, the Islamic world had yet to reach its political and cultural peak. The Mongol invasions had been devastating. However, by the 15th century not only had the Islamic world recovered from the invasions, but it had also begun to take great strides forward. With the rise of three new empires the majority of the regions of Islam now had dynamic political leadership.

At the height of their power these three states ruled over a vast area stretching from what is known today as Bangladesh west to modern-day Algeria. In the east, ruling over the Indian subcontinent, was the Mughal Empire with its capital in Delhi. In Iran the Safavid dynasty arose to establish a new Shii state ruling from Isfahan. And beginning in the middle of the 14th century a Turkish state known as the Ottoman Empire arose in Anatolia. In time, the Ottomans would control most of North Africa and the Middle East, all of Anatolia, and much of southeastern Europe.

The Sultan Ahmed mosque, also known as the Blue Mosque, was built in Istanbul between 1609 and 1616. In 1453 one Ottoman ruler, Mehmet II, laid siege to Constantinople, the capital of the once-great Byzantine Empire. The city fell and the new Muslim rulers renamed it Istanbul.

The Taj Mahal is one of the best-known examples of Islamic architecture. Located in Agra, India, the building is a mausoleum for Mumtaz Mahal, the favorite wife of the Mughal emperor Shah Jahan. Construction began in 1632.

The rulers of these three empires were not spiritual guides or teachers in the way Muhammad had been. Their role, at least in theoretical terms, was to uphold the Islamic faith and to see that the lands of Islam were well defended against both internal and external threats. In this way, like the caliphs of old, the Mughal, Safavid, and Ottoman rulers had both political and religious responsibilities.

ARCHITECTURE AND CULTURE OF THE EMPIRES

The political power of these dynasties coincided with cultural and economic activity throughout the Islamic world. Like the Mughal rulers, the Safavids also took a keen interest in religious and cultural matters. Abbas I, the greatest of the Safavid leaders, ruled from 1588 to 1629 and did much to promote Iranian art and architecture. Along with magnificent buildings erected in Isfahan, the capital, Iranian artists produced works of calligraphy and miniature painting as well as manuscript illustration. Others in the dynasty also encouraged the work of the religious and legal scholars, many of whom worked as government functionaries in schools, mosques, and cultural centers.

The achievements of the Ottoman sultans were no less brilliant. At their peak of prestige they provided an atmosphere in which scholars, artists, musicians, architects, and poets all flourished. The beautiful mosques and other buildings of present-day Istanbul attest to the cultural environment fostered by these rulers.

COMMERCE, RELIGION, AND POLITICS

This period also witnessed a great deal of commercial activity. All three dynasties were able to provide the areas under their control with political and economic stability. Throughout this period merchants bought and sold a great variety of goods—from expensive spices, clothes, and jewels to basic foodstuffs such as rice and wheat. This commerce was carried out within each of the empires as well as across frontiers, as great trade caravans and ocean fleets crisscrossed the regions of the Middle East and southern Asia.

This was also a period when the religious scholars, or ulama (meaning "learned ones"), became deeply involved in a wide range of activities—largely with the blessings of the political rulers. The religious scholars served the community as teachers, prayer leaders, and spiritual guides. Some ulama served as local political leaders, voicing the wishes and grievances of their followers to the state. The governments in Isfahan, Istanbul, and Delhi all recognized the value of having control over these religious figures. As a result they employed growing numbers of these men in the government bureaucracy.

Eventually the ulama became a divided group. Whereas the top scholars—those men with good positions in the bureaucracy—supported the state, other ulama kept their distance from the government. In Iran especially, the lower-ranked members of this religious community refused to serve the state. Some of these men became critics of the political establishment, while many others stayed completely out of politics. Those few who spoke out won the support of the general public.

Interior of the Sultan Hassan Mosque, Cairo, Egypt. The flight of steps leads to the *minbar,* where the Friday sermon is given to the congregation.

CONQUEST, EDUCATION, AND PREACHING

During the 15th to 18th centuries Islam spread further afield in both Asia and Africa. The spread of Islam took place in a variety of ways. Conquests brought new areas under Islamic rule. For example areas of Central Asia, India, and Central Africa were conquered at different times by Muslim forces. Education and preaching by Muslim missionaries, teachers, holy men, and scholars spread Islam to newly conquered areas and to remote parts of previously established Islamic territories. Often these were charismatic men who won people over to Islam through the force of their character and message. Just as often such missionaries and teachers worked within populations that had long been under Islamic rule but had not yet converted. In Anatolia, for example, under the Ottomans, many Christians converted to Islam.

Just as important was the role played by merchants who were active during this period. In coastal areas from East Africa to the islands of Indonesia, merchants established contacts with local populations. These social exchanges led to the establishment of small communities where missionaries, among others, would come to settle. In this way Islam gradually spread, for example, to the interior regions of Indonesia and Africa.

THE END OF THE EMPIRES

As with all empires the days of prestige and power came to an end as strife slowly sapped the strength of all three of the dynasties. What were once dynamic states slowly became hollow shells that finally collapsed under the pressures of both internal upheavals and external threats. The Safavid and Mughal states disappeared by the 19th century, and the Ottomans held on until the early part of the 20th century before finally vanishing.

By the 18th century, however, Islam had established itself throughout vast areas of Africa and Asia. In many of these regions Muslims were the dominant majority. Of course differences remained great in languages, local customs and values, eating habits and dress, art and music, and economic systems from one region to the next. However despite these differences strong and lasting bonds developed to tie the disparate Islamic regions together. As Muslims all the peoples of these regions worshipped the one God, Allah, and venerated his messenger, Muhammad. All prayed facing the sacred city of Mecca, and all carried out the other specific rituals expected of Muslims. And of course all sought guidance from Islam's great book—the Quran.

CHAPTER 4

QURAN, HADITH, AND THE LAW

Muslims believe that the text of the Quran is the literal Word of God—revealed to Muhammad during his lifetime, written down by his followers under his supervision, and put into book form soon after his death. For this reason the Quran provides the foundation and guiding spirit of Islam.

THE WORD OF GOD

Muslims become acquainted with the Quran at a young age and many continue to study it throughout their lives. Verses of the book are recited into the ears of babies, and as soon as Muslim children are old enough to speak they begin memorizing and reciting Quranic verses. Muslim children learn to read and write by reciting the book and by copying out verses by hand. As young Muslims approach adulthood they learn to use the book in prayer. The attachment to the Quran continues until the last days of a Muslim's life, when sections of the book are often read to the dying. Finally, following Islamic tradition, selected passages of the Quran are recited over the grave of a deceased Muslim.

A Muslim family studying the Quran at an Islamic center in Indonesia. Today the majority of Muslims are not native speakers of Arabic and therefore the Quran is made available to them in translation. However, any translation of the Quran ceases to be the literal word of Allah.

The Arabic Language

Public recitations of the Quran are always conducted in Arabic, as it is believed that God revealed the Quran to Muhammad in Arabic: "We have revealed it, a Quran in Arabic, so that you might understand" (12.2). For this reason even the many Muslims who do not speak or read Arabic view that language with great respect.

Memorization and recital of the Quran are highly valued activities in the Islamic world. Most Muslim children learn portions of the Quran by heart and use them continually in prayer and on other occasions. Some Muslims go on to memorize the entire book—an act that earns them the respect of their communities. Muslims also place great value in the recitation of the Quran. Throughout the Islamic world Muslims gather to hear the book recited and show great appreciation for those with particularly well-trained voices.

It is difficult to convey the depth of appreciation and attachment that Muslims feel toward the Quran. For Muslims the book is a unique event in the history of humankind. It is often described as the one true miracle brought by Muhammad. It is thought that since the Quran represents the Word of God, it is a perfect work. Like God it is eternal and unchangeable.

A British Muslim girl quietly reading the Quran in Arabic. The Quran teaches that its words were sent down to Muhammad from God in the Arabic language.

THE MESSAGE OF THE QURAN

According to Islamic tradition and the Quran itself, the Quran is the last in a series of revelations sent to the world by God. Among his messengers were Moses and the other Hebrew prophets, who brought the Torah, and Jesus Christ, whose followers documented his life and his teachings in the New Testament of the Bible. Like them Muhammad was the bearer of a divine message—the Quran.

Therefore Muslims do not reject the earlier messages brought by Moses, Jesus, and the other prophets who came before Muhammad. On the contrary the Islamic tradition views these earlier prophets and their messages with great esteem. However the Quran teaches that over time both the Jewish and Christian scriptures have been corrupted by the men and women who have tried to interpret them.

For example the Jews and the Christians are criticized in the Quran for having claimed to be a divinely chosen people. The Quran states that only God will decide who, if anyone, is to be chosen and for what reasons. The Christians are also criticized for having thought of Christ as divine. In the view of Muslims this is to say that God shares his divine nature or that God has a divine partner. This idea contradicts one of the most fundamental Islamic principles—the absolute oneness of God.

The Quran condemns any individual or group that tries to associate any object or being with God. Muslims use the term *shirk* (associating anything with God) for such an act, which they believe is the one unforgivable sin that humans can commit. Muslims believe that Christians commit an act of *shirk* when they claim that Jesus is divine.

Muslims believe that the role of the Quran is to correct the errors and false ideas that men and women have added to

SURAS AND AYAS

The Quran is made up of 114 chapters known as *suras*, each of which is made up of a varying number of verses, called *ayas*. The longest chapter contains 286 verses, the shortest only three. The longer chapters are known as the Medinan chapters because it is believed they were revealed to Muhammad after his arrival in Medina, following his journey from Mecca. The shorter chapters are believed to have been revealed earlier, in Mecca, and are called the *Meccan suras*.

God's earlier revelations. As the final revelation from God, it is believed to be the most perfect. It was sent to warn humanity that the earlier revelations had been corrupted and to bring people back to the true religion.

GOD, HUMANKIND, HEAVEN, AND HELL

According to Islamic tradition God is first of all merciful, ready to forgive the sinner as long as that person repents and turns back to the worship of God and a truly religious life. God is also generous. The Quran speaks often about the bounty of the natural world given to humanity by God. It says, "God is He Who created the heavens and the earth and sent down water from the clouds, then brought forth with it fruits to sustain you." (14.32)

The greatest proofs of God's mercy and compassion, however, are the prophets and the revelation, particularly the prophet Muhammad and the Quran. These provide men and women with the guidance they require to make their way through the world and ultimately to salvation. The revelation and the teachings of Muhammad accomplish several tasks: They warn humanity of the evils of sin, they provide knowledge of God and of the proper ways to worship, and they describe the rewards that await the person who follows the revelation and Muhammad's example.

MASTER OF THE DAY OF JUDGMENT

However God is also the Master of the Day of Judgment, whose power and justice are as great as his mercy. For those sinners who repent God will show forgiveness, but for those sinners who persist in their corrupt ways God will be unforgiving. One verse in the Quran says that the sinner who attempts to win forgiveness with all the wealth of the world, and even twice that, will fail. God will review their lives on the Day of Judgment and find them unrepentant. Their reward will be the fires of hell.

The Quran offers vivid descriptions of both heaven and hell. In hell sinners suffer from both physical and mental anguish. While despair and fear fill their hearts and minds, their bodies are tortured with fire and molten metals. A very different experience is promised for those who are saved. Heaven is described in the Quran as a place of rich gardens with running springs, where the saved will delight in the best of food and drink and the companionship of beautiful young men and women.

In hell the sinners join Satan and his followers. The story of Satan, who is known as Iblis in the Islamic tradition, is one of the most vivid parts of the Quran. It begins with an affirmation of the special relationship that exists between humankind and God. God created people to serve as his representatives on earth. At the moment of creation God summoned the angels to inform them of humanity's special quality. He ordered them to bow down before the first of humans, Adam, but Iblis angrily refused.

When Iblis refused to bow down before Adam, God cast him out of heaven for disobeying the divine command:

Then all the angels bowed together, except Iblis, who refused to join those who were bowing. God said: "Oh, Iblis, why are you not among those who are upon their knees?" He said: "I am not going to kneel before a being formed out of clay, of shaped mud." God said: "Then leave here, you are cast out, and indeed you are cursed until the Day of Judgment." He said: "My Lord, spare me until the Day of Resurrection." God said: "You may

SPIRITUAL CREATURES

According to the Quran, in both heaven and hell humans will be joined by spirits created by God. The spiritual creatures of heaven are the angels. Created out of light, their role is to serve as messengers between God and humanity, delivering the divine revelation to those chosen by God. It was the angel Gabriel who brought the revelation from God to Muhammad in the cave at Hira. Below the angels are the jinn, who are made of fire and who can be either good or bad. Like human beings, these fiery spirits will be judged by God at the end of time and sent to either heaven or hell. In the period before Islam the jinn were thought to inhabit rocks and trees. With the establishment of Islam belief in the jinn was incorporated into the new religion, seeing them as intermediaries between humanity and the angels but not always to be trusted or believed!

join those waiting for that appointed day." He said: "Since you have made evil of me, I will certainly make the world attractive to those on earth, and I will make evil of all of them, except those of them who are your sincere followers." God said: "This is the path that leads directly to me. As for my followers, you will have no influence over them except those who go astray to follow you, and surely Hell will be the place for them." (15.30–43)

HUMAN RESPONSIBILITIES

The Quran clearly states that God expects humans to perform the rituals of Islam and read the Quran. However it also provides guidelines for living life as a Muslim. According to the Quran human beings are individually responsible for their own actions and thoughts. Consequently the decision to follow the true path of God, to live a sincerely religious life, is up to each person. Those who choose to do so will win God's mercy, and those who do not will earn only his anger.

THE MUSLIM COMMUNITY AND THE QURAN

The devout Muslim is not only an individual but also a member of the Islamic community. That community has the responsibility to follow God's will, which means to uphold the teachings of the Quran. As the Quran says, God made the Muslims into a particular community, or *umma,* just as he had earlier done with the Jews and Christians. He expects that community to act as an example to all other communities.

GUIDING THE COMMUNITY

To guide the community the Quran provides regulations that every Muslim is expected to follow. These include not only the ritual duties of prayer but also rules regarding inheritance, marriage, and other aspects of life. Over the course of Islamic history these rules have become the basis of Islamic law. The Quran says that the goal of the Muslim community is to create a just society. So the Quran not only teaches human beings about God, Muhammad, and the revelation but also serves as a guide to the community of Muslims on how to follow God from day to day.

A page from an 18th-century Turkish Quran decorated with geometric patterns. The Quran contains many passages that require much study before their meaning becomes clear. Since Muslims throughout the ages have sought guidance from the Quran, it has always been important for them to know what the book is teaching. As a result those who study the Quran are looked to by other Muslims for guidance. Often these people become teachers in their local communities.

Studying and explaining the Quran became, very early on, an important branch of Islamic education and intellectual life. *Tafsir* is the term used by Muslims for Quranic interpretation or explanation. In the ninth and 10th centuries Muslim scholars spent years studying the verses of the Quran. The best of these scholars produced multivolume works—still used today in universities throughout the Islamic world—in which they laid out their detailed interpretations. Perhaps the most famous of these works, *Mukhtasar tarikh al rusul wal muluk wal khulafa*, was written in the early 10th century by a scholar in Baghdad named Abu Jafar Muhammad ibn Jarir al-Tabari (d. 923).

LIFE AND TEACHINGS OF MUHAMMAD

Although the Quran embodies the teachings of Islam, there is another source of guidance Muslims look to as well—the life and teachings of Muhammad. No individual is viewed with the same awe and respect by Muslims as is Muhammad ibn Abd Allah. In countless biographies and poems Muslims have spoken of their profound attachment to the prophet. He is revered by Muslims for his special relationship to God. Like the prophets before him he was selected to bring the divine message to humanity. However Muhammad is thought to have been closer to God than were any of the other prophets. He was the one chosen to bring the Quran, God's last revelation, to humanity. For that reason his relationship to God was unique.

MUHAMMAD AND HADITH

Muhammad is also revered by Muslims for having lived a remarkable life. A gifted teacher, Muhammad inspired his listeners. A great political leader, Muhammad turned a small group of followers into a powerful community, the foundation of an expanding empire. A skilled military chief, he led his followers to victory against more powerful enemies, eventually gaining control of the entire Arabian Peninsula.

For all these reasons it was not long before Muhammad was seen by his followers as a model human being. For them and for the generations of Muslims after them, he became the example for all Muslims to follow—not only an exemplary human being, but even incapable of error of any kind.

THE HADITH

Even during Muhammad's lifetime Muslims began to collect stories of his activities and teachings. His closest followers—those who had observed Muhammad on a daily basis for years—passed on these stories to others after his death. These accounts, known as hadith, grew very popular and soon were circulating throughout the Islamic community.

As the hadith began to circulate through the community, Muslims listened with great interest. These reports were passed on from person to person, community to community, in both written and oral form through the centuries. From the hadith Muslims learned about Muhammad's accomplishments as a military and political leader as well as details of his private life. For instance there are accounts of Muhammad's methods of battle and diplomacy as well as descriptions of his religious activities and family life. No Muslim could ever hope to be like Muhammad in every way, but many Muslims believe that if they strive to follow Muhammad's example, they will live a pious and meaningful life.

FINDING THE TRUE HADITH

By the time Islam had spread beyond the Arabian Peninsula it became obvious to many in the Islamic community that most of these reports about Muhammad were fabrications, that they had been created after Muhammad's death by members of the community who claimed that they had heard the reports from someone who had recorded them in the time of the prophet. Very often those who made up these reports were well-meaning Muslims who thought that their act of fabrication was a sign of their reverence for Muhammad. Others had created new hadith in an attempt to put forth their own answers to problems facing the early Muslim community. While no one was punished for this activity, it became clear that the fabricated reports would have to be weeded out. After all, if the community was going to use the hadith as a source of guidance, it would have to be sure that only the true hadith were being used.

In order to find the true hadith Muslim scholars began to examine large numbers of these reports. Since the empire had grown so large scholars often had to travel vast distances in order to collect the many accounts. Gradually the scholars were able to distinguish the real hadith from the

DEMAND FOR THE HADITH

Within 200 years of Muhammad's death the numbers of hadith (accounts of Muhammad's activities and teachings) circulating around the Islamic community probably were in the hundreds of thousands. By that time the Islamic Empire had spread well beyond the limits of the Arabian Peninsula. In the areas conquered by the Muslim armies large numbers of people had converted to Islam. Like those before them these new Muslims were eager to learn about Muhammad and his teachings. This further increased the demand for the hadith.

fabricated ones. Out of this exhausting effort came a number of collections of hadith that were considered reliable.

As time went on six of these collections were shown preference by the scholarly community of Islam and became the standard works of hadith—still read today by students and scholars in universities throughout the Islamic world.

THE LAW OF GOD

For Muslims the sharia, or Islamic law, is the divine plan for the Islamic community. It lays out the regulations and duties that all Muslims are expected to follow during the course of their lives, including the rituals that Muslims are expected to perform when worshipping Allah as well as the regulations for behavior with one's family and in society.

The sharia developed from the deeply felt needs of the early Muslims. The conquests had transformed the small community in Medina into a powerful empire. For many Muslims, however, the riches of the empire were only of secondary importance. The first priority was the assurance of a moral Islamic community. If it was to follow the Word of God and the teachings of Muhammad, these Muslims said, it needed a body of Islamic law.

From the eighth to the start of the 10th century scholars of Islam worked at the difficult process of developing this body of law. One problem they faced was that many passages in the Quran were interpreted in different ways by different scholars, resulting in arguments and disputes. The Quran moreover did not contain answers—even partial answers—to all the questions they faced. In those cases where even the hadith did not provide answers

A man praying using *mishaba*, prayer beads. There are 99 prayer beads corresponding to the 99 names of God. By repeating these names, such as the Compassionate and the Merciful, Muslims are brought closer to God.

the scholars were obliged to come to a solution by using their own opinions, guided as closely as possible by the principles of the Quran and hadith.

By the beginning of the 10th century the legal experts had reached their goal: The basic elements of the sharia were in place. This code of regulations, set out in legal manuals written by the various scholars and their students, showed that the disagreements among the different groups of legal scholars had not disappeared. On certain issues of law, such as how divorce between a husband and wife could be achieved and how the property of a deceased person was to be divided among the person's heirs, the scholars had reached conflicting conclusions about what the Quran and hadith permitted. These differences led to the emergence of various schools of Islamic law.

THE SCHOOLS OF LAW

The schools all developed in the same way: A gifted scholar would set out his ideas in his classes and writings; his students would refine these and pass them on to their students, who would in turn do the same. In the early period a number of these schools came into being, but most of them dissolved quickly. The few that survived were named after the men around whom the schools had first formed.

HANAFI SCHOOL

The two oldest Sunni legal schools are called Hanafi and Maliki. The former was named after Abu Hanifa (d. 767), a legal scholar who lived and worked in the Iraqi city of Kufah. He acquired a reputation among scholars for his liberal views on the law and for his great intelligence. Abu Hanifa used legal precedents other than those found in the hadith to expand Islamic law and advised that extreme Quranic punishments should be used rarely. Some of the greatest legal scholars of the following generation were his students. The Hanafi school is currently dominant in India, Central Asia, Turkey, and parts of Egypt.

MALIKI SCHOOL

The Maliki school took its name from Malik ibn Anas (d. 796), a scholar from the city of Medina—the first capital of the Islamic Empire and the center of vigorous work by legal and religious scholars. Malik was one of the most highly respected of these men. The Ummayad caliphs had claimed that laws could be made without reference to the Quran, but Malik ibn Anas overturned this right and once again placed emphasis on the importance of the hadith. He is known to the present day for his dedication to collecting hadith and for writing the *al-Muwatta*—one of the most influential early books on the law. The Maliki school is currently dominant in North and Central Africa.

SHAFII SCHOOL

Perhaps the greatest legal scholar in Islamic history was Muhammad ibn Idris al-Shafii, who gave his name to the Shafii school of law, which is currently followed in Malaysia, southern Arabia, and East Africa. He was born in Palestine and studied in various parts of the Middle East, including Medina, where he studied under the great Malik ibn Anas. He then taught in Baghdad and later Egypt, where he died in 819. Al-Shafii laid out his ideas on the law in the *Risala*—one of the most renowned books of the early period of Islam.

In his book al-Shafii argued persuasively that after the Quran the most important source for legal scholars to use in reaching their decisions was the hadith. It was to a great extent because of this argument that the hadith became so highly regarded by all Muslims. With al-Shafii's work the

Muslims in the courtyard of Vakil mosque, Shiraz, Iran. Mosques throughout the Islamic world are used for prayer, study, and contemplation. During the month-long fast of Ramadan it is common for Muslims, usually men, to spend long hours in the mosque reading, praying, and quietly conversing.

stature of Muhammad rose to new heights. Like Abu Hanifa, al-Shafii attracted many fine students, some of whom went on to contribute to the development of Islamic law.

HANBALI SCHOOL

The last of the Sunni legal schools to emerge was the Hanbali school—named after Ahmad ibn Hanbal (d. 855), who was a younger contemporary of al-Shafii in Baghdad. Early on ibn Hanbal acquired the reputation for being outspoken and very conservative. Frequently he had bitter arguments with other scholars over a variety of religious and legal issues. He even became involved in an angry dispute with the court and at one point was arrested and beaten for his opinions. This helped strengthen his following among students and younger scholars who shared his views. Today the only area where the Hanbali school is dominant is the modern state of Saudi Arabia.

SHII LAW—THE JAFIRI SCHOOL

Besides the schools of legal thought in the Sunni Muslim community, there is the Shii law school, which is known as the Jafiri school. It was named after a great Shii scholar who lived and taught in Medina and later in Baghdad: Jafar al-Sadiq. In his early career al-Sadiq lived a quiet life, writing and holding classes for his students. In 750 the Abbasids swept into power, and in a short time the quiet of al-Sadiq's life was shattered.

Al-Sadiq was by that time one of the leading members of the Shii community. This status was not entirely to his liking. The new Abbasid caliphs from the very start of their rule viewed the Shia as political rivals and therefore kept a close eye on al-Sadiq and other Shii leaders. Although al-Sadiq had always been careful to stay out of politics—partly for fear that he would end up beheaded like Shii leader Husayn—the second Abbasid caliph, al-Mansur, ordered al-Sadiq arrested on several occasions. Al-Sadiq died in the year 765 and it was believed by many that he was poisoned on the orders of the caliph. For the Shia, his death would drive one more wedge between the two Muslim communities.

CHAPTER 5

THE VARIETY OF RELIGIOUS LIFE IN ISLAM

The division of the Islamic community into the Sunni and Shii traditions began with the deaths of Ali (Prophet Muhammad's cousin, son-in-law, and the fourth caliph) in 661 and his son Husayn in 680. Deprived of their leaders the Shia grew frustrated as the Umayyads took over the caliphate. Despite the loss of Ali and Husayn many of the Shia remained loyal to the Alid family.

The title given by the Shia to Ali, his two sons, and a select group of men who came after them was imam. Following Husayn's brutal murder the Shia agreed that the position of imam should go to a member of the Alid family. But which one?

A number of the Shia argued that the new imam was now Husayn's son, also named Ali, the only one of Husayn's male offspring to survive the massacre at Karbala in 680. Ali, known also as Zayn al-Abidin, was then a respected scholar esteemed for his deep piety. However others of the Shia had another choice in mind. This disagreement led to a division within the Shii community. Although a number remained faithful to Ali, the son of

Muslim girls greeting each other. Muslim women traditionally dress modestly. As long as they stay within religious guidelines, the type of clothes that are worn may vary according to cultural tradition and personal choice.

Husayn, others threw their loyalty behind a third son of Ali ibn Abi Talib, a man named Muhammad ibn al-Hanafiyya.

When ibn al-Hanafiyya died in 700 and Ali Zayn al Abidin died in 712, once again, the Shia—including the followers of ibn al-Hanafiyya and Ali Zayn al Abidin—faced the problem of finding a new imam. As before they could not agree on which Alid to choose as their next leader. A number of small Shii groups appeared, each with its own candidate for imam. This pattern of disagreement over the successor of a deceased imam would repeat itself frequently over the next 200 years. Most of these groups were small and disappeared quickly. Only a handful of them survived this early period.

THE SHII BRANCHES

Of these various branches of the Shia, the earliest to emerge was the Zaydi tradition. Zayd ibn Ali, after whom this group is named, was the son of Ali Zayn al-Abidin. Unlike his father Zayd was willing to fight for the rights of the Alid family. In 740 he organized a rebellion in Kufah against the Umayyads. As with Husayn years earlier, the Kufans promised their support to Zayd. Once again, at the crucial moment the Kufans backed out. The Umayyad soldiers overwhelmed Zayd's followers, killing Zayd in the process.

Despite Zayd's death his followers remained active. Led by other members of the Alid family one group of Zaydis settled in northern Iran, where they established a small state that survived into the 11th century. Other Zaydis made their way to Yemen in southwestern Arabia. The state they established there would have a long, frequently violent history throughout which the Zaydis maintained their presence. In the early part of the 20th century the leaders of this Zaydi community were able to create an independent state that lasted into the 1960s before succumbing to revolution.

THE ISMAILIS

The history of another sect of the Shia was no less eventful. The Ismaili Shia emerged after the death of the man they looked to as their imam. Ismail ibn Jafar was the son of the famous Shii scholar Jafar al-Sadiq, a great-grandson of the famous Husayn. Although he died at a fairly young age Ismail was seen by a number of Shiis as their imam. They transferred their loyalties to his son Muhammad ibn Ismail and then to his descendants.

The Ismailis, like the Zaydis, showed a great deal of resourcefulness in spreading their doctrines. Organized in small cells Ismaili activists moved into various regions to form small communities. The movement broke apart in the ninth century when one of its leading activists, Ubayd Allah, claimed that he was the new imam. Rejected by the other Ismailis, he and his followers went to the area of North Africa known today as Tunisia. In a mountainous area Ubayd Allah and his men organized a small army. They then overthrew the Abbasid governor who controlled the area. The result was the birth of the Fatimid dynasty in 969.

THE TWELVER SHIA

The most influential and numerous Shii groups is known in Arabic as the Ithna Ashariyya and in English as the Twelver

The Druze

In the 11th century a new movement emerged within the Ismaili sect that came to be known as the Druze. Today the Druze number roughly 300,000 and live in Syria, Israel, and Lebanon. Many Muslims believe that the Druze hold ideas that violate the basic tenets of Islam and for this reason should not be considered part of the Islamic community.

The Alawi

The Nusayri community, also known as the Alawi, is another small Shii group that emerged during the medieval period. This group, which continues to exist today, has lived for centuries in small villages in northern Syria. The present ruler of Syria, Hafiz al-Asad, is an Alawi, as are members of his government and top officers of the military. There is much opposition within Syria today to the Asad regime; one reason for this is the resentment felt by the Sunni majority over being ruled by a minority that holds certain different religious beliefs such as the human body being a trap entombing divine souls and that souls transmigrate into human or animal form.

Shia. Today the Twelvers form a majority in Iran and are present in large numbers in Lebanon, Kuwait, and Iraq. With little doubt the most significant member of this sect in recent years was the man who led the 1979 Islamic Revolution in Iran, the Ayatollah Khomeini. Before his death in June 1989 he had become one of the most controversial figures in recent world history.

Muslims praying in the direction of Mecca in the Islamic Center of America. The Islamic Center was established in Detroit in 1963 and the current building was completed in 2005. Many members of the community are Shiis but the center is open to all Muslims.

THE TWELVE IMAMS

As the name of the sect indicates the Twelvers believe that the position of imam passed from Ali ibn Abi Talib down through a chain of 11 other men, all descendants of Ali's family. Among them were Ali ibn Abi Talib and his two sons, Hasan and Husayn, who were the second and third imams after their father. The fourth imam was Ali Zayn al-Abidin and the sixth was the renowned Jafar al-Sadiq. Famous for his deep piety and brilliant scholarship, he was responsible for developing many of the doctrines of the Twelver sect. These doctrines centered on the figure of the imam. According to the Twelvers the imams possessed certain distinguishing characteristics.

DIVINE INSPIRATION

First the imams were divinely inspired. Like Muhammad they are believed to have had a close relationship with God. In the books of Twelver scholars the imams are referred to as The Proof of God or The Sign of God. These titles are used to show that the imams are God's representatives on earth and that devotion to the imams is required of all.

Unlike Muhammad the imams did not carry a divine message to humankind. However insofar as the imams were the providers of spiritual guidance, they were considered the direct heirs to Muhammad's legacy. Some Twelver writers have described the imams as having been created out of the same substance as Muhammad. The substance is described as a brilliant light created by God before the creation of the world. From this divine light God is believed to have created Muhammad and the imams as well as Fatima, the prophet Muhammad's daughter, the wife of Ali ibn Abi Talib, and the mother of Hasan and Husayn.

APPOINTMENT BY IMAMS

The Twelvers also believed that each of the imams was appointed by the imam

Fatima

As the daughter of the prophet Muhammad, the wife of Ali ibn Abi Talib, and the mother of Hasan and Husayn, Fatima is highly revered not only by the Twelvers but by other Shiis as well.

before him. Just as Ali had appointed Hasan, Hasan appointed Husayn, and so on. This idea grew from the belief that Muhammad had chosen Ali as his successor in a sermon he gave at the end of his life. In his sermon Muhammad reportedly told the Muslims gathered before him that upon his death they were to follow Ali. Although Sunni Muslims deny this ever took place, the Shia believe that it did, and for them it is an event of great significance.

POSSESSING KNOWLEDGE AND WITHOUT ERROR

The imams, according to the Twelvers, possessed two other characteristics as well. First they were incapable of error or sin. Second the imams were in possession of a special body of knowledge, which they received from God through Muhammad, and which allowed them to serve as the spiritual and political leaders of the community.

These were characteristics possessed by all 12 of the imams. Clearly in the eyes of the Shia they were unique and remarkable human beings. Of the 12 there was one who stood out among all the others: the Twelfth Imam.

THE ONE GUIDED BY GOD

The term used for the Hidden Imam is *al-Mahdi,* or "the one guided by God." In his role as the Mahdi the Twelfth Imam is expected to bring a new social order to the world—an eternal age of justice in which the sufferings of the Shii community will end. As we have seen, the Shia were a minority in the Islamic community and too often a persecuted minority. They had seen their leaders killed and imprisoned; moreover, early in their history they had attempted several revolts against the rule of the Umayyad and Abbasid caliphs, only to see these revolts harshly put down. It is believed that with his armies of angels and followers rising up with him on that chosen day, the Hidden Imam will finally end the suffering of the Shii community. He will then rule with justice and wisdom over that community until the Day of Judgment, when God will decide the fate of every being.

THE TWELFTH IMAM

In 874 Hasan al-Askari, the Eleventh Imam, suddenly died in the city of Samarra—then the capital of the Abbasid caliphate. Just as had happened after the deaths of the other imams, the Shii community argued over who was the successor to al-Askari. Some said it was his brother Jafar; others disagreed. The Twelvers had their own opinion.

They insisted that al-Askari had an infant son whom he had chosen to succeed him. This was the first that many in the Shii community had heard of the boy, so they reacted with skepticism. How were they to know he existed? The response came that to reveal his identity was to risk having the boy and the whole Shii community attacked by the Abbasid authorities. While the Shia were less politically active than they had been in earlier periods, they were still viewed with suspicion by the Abbasids. For this reason it was considered unwise to reveal the identity of the new imam.

While many expressed doubts about this mysterious child, the majority of Shiis slowly came to accept the idea that he had become the new imam and that he was in hiding until some future time. Thus he was given the title of the Hidden Imam. The scholars of the Twelver community taught that he had gone into hiding in a small cave in Samarra. Today Shiis still gather in the small mosque located over this cave to pray for his return.

THE RECKONING DAY

Following the disappearance of the Twelfth Imam many in the Twelver community began to wonder when he would come out of hiding. When asked, the Twelver scholars said that the Twelfth Imam would emerge from hiding when he was summoned by God; in other words at the end of time. On that Last Day, the scholars explained, the Hidden Imam will reappear in a burst of celestial light. He will stand at the head of an army of angels and of all the Shiis who over the centuries followed the imams faithfully. He will be wearing Muhammad's sandals and ring, and in his hand he will wield Muhammad's sword. His destinations will be Mecca, then Medina, and then the rest of the world. In each of these places he will promise eternal life to those who were faithful to the imams. And with great violence he will then turn against those who oppressed the imams and the community of Shia.

DISAGREEMENT BETWEEN THE SUNNIS AND THE SHIIS

Held dear by the Twelver Shia these ideas about the imams were never accepted by the Sunni community. In fact such notions were a major cause of the division between the two communities.

For the Shiis political and religious leadership could only come from one source: the imams. The Twelfth Imam would eventually return to right all the wrongs of the world. For these reasons the imams—and they alone—could serve as the proper leaders of the community.

The Sunnis had a different idea of leadership. They respected the imams as men of great learning but they could not accept that the imams were inspired by God. Nor could they agree that the imams were the direct heirs of Muhammad. For the Sunnis the leaders of the community were the caliphs.

It was not believed that the caliphs were divinely inspired or in possession of special knowledge of any kind. They were simply human beings chosen to lead the community in this world: to defend the community from internal and external enemies and to uphold the sharia. They were never considered a source of religious guidance in the way the imams were by the Shia.

THE PATH TO SALVATION

Another major disagreement between the Shiis and the Sunnis was over the idea of salvation. The Islamic community, it was believed, would win God's mercy on the Day of Judgment only if the community as a whole lived according to God's law. For the Sunnis the sharia, as the embodiment of God's law, had to be respected and followed by all. The caliphs were there only to defend the sharia and to protect the community, not to lead the community to salvation. Only the entire Islamic community working as a whole could achieve this goal.

For the Shia the quest for salvation lay not with the community but with the imams. Without them it could never hope to win God's mercy; only the imams could lead the Islamic community along the right path.

ULAMA—GUIDANCE AND LEADERSHIP

During the years that each of the imams lived and taught within the community, the Shia could turn to them for guidance. This changed, however, when the Twelfth Imam disappeared. The Shia now faced a troubling question. If the imams were the only true guides of the community, then what was to happen when the last of the imams was no longer present? If no imam was present, then what was to prevent the Shia from losing faith in the imams and in their religious beliefs? And who was to speak for the community in times of trouble?

Answers to these questions came from the scholars of the Twelver community: the ulama. They argued that they would carry out the functions of the Hidden Imam until such time as God decides that the Hidden Imam should return. This did not mean the scholars were claiming themselves as equal to the imams. Rather they were acting as caretakers and would represent the imam until his return, when they would hand over these responsibilities to him.

A small mosque on the banks of the Tigris River in Baghdad, Iraq. The tall tower of the minaret can be seen on the skyline and is used by the muezzin to call Muslims to prayer.

These ideas were developed over a long period, from roughly the end of the 11th century into the 19th century and up to the present day. The Twelver ulama, especially the leading members, became very influential. These men at the top of a hierarchy of scholars wielded a great deal of power—especially in Iran, where a large proportion of the populace eventually converted to the Twelver Shia sect.

For a time the political power of the Twelver scholars was limited, mainly because Iran was under the rule of Sunni leaders who wanted to keep power out of the hands of the Shia. This changed in the 16th century with the rise of the Shii Safavid dynasty, which gave the ulama the opportunity to influence political decisions. However the ulama disagreed among themselves over how involved in politics they should become. Moreover despite their acceptance of Twelver doctrines the leaders of the new dynasty were concerned that the ulama would gain too much power; they determined not to let that happen.

In the meantime the ulama continued to debate the question of their involvement in politics. Some said that politics should be avoided and that the ulama should concentrate on religious activities. Others argued that by increasing their political involvement the ulama could work toward limiting the corrupt activities of the state. Still others maintained that political activity was fine but not if it meant serving the government. The role of the ulama in their view should be to support the state when it ruled justly but to attack it when it became tyrannical. Above all, they said, the religious leadership should maintain its independence from the government.

THE QAJAR DYNASTY

While this debate among the ulama continued, Iran's political landscape changed. The Safavids were overthrown in the middle of the 18th century. The new rulers, the Qajars, were also Shiis; like the Safavids, however, they were wary of the ulama becoming too powerful and therefore sought to keep the scholarly community at bay. To do so they placed a number of ulama in government positions. Although on the surface this move seemed contrary to the rulers' purpose, it actually served them quite well. Through these appointed officials they were able to keep a close eye on the ulama and their activities. The appointments also enabled Iran's rulers to claim they had the support of the scholarly community. The tensions between the state and Iran's religious leaders remained, however.

THE PAHLAVI DYNASTY

At the start of the 20th century the Qajars were replaced by a new power: the Pahlavi dynasty. The founder of the dynasty was a violent-tempered officer named Reza Khan (1878–1944), who set out to create a centralized state in Iran. To control the religious community Reza Khan instituted policies that strictly limited the activities of the ulama.

For a time Reza Khan was successful in controlling Iran's religious leaders. His policies, however, angered many Iranians. As Reza Khan, and then his son Muhammad, continued to pursue these policies hostility to the dynasty grew. By the 1960s these tensions would reach the point of explosion.

THE ASCETICS OF ISLAM

The division of the early Islamic community into different groups had come out of conflicts over matters of religion and politics. At the same time the early community was facing another kind of conflict—not of sword and fire but of spiritual beliefs.

The successes of the early Islamic community had been startling. In a relatively short time the once small and vulnerable community had spread beyond Arabia into the regions of the Middle East, Central Asia, and North Africa. With the conquest of these large territories had also come new levels of wealth. This was especially true of the Muslim military and political elite, who gained control of large cities, most of which were important commercial centers. Thus they were able to expand and benefit from trade. They also accumulated wealth by imposing heavy taxes on the people of these conquered cities. As they prospered the elites of Islamic society, including the caliphs, lived in great luxury.

REJECTING RICHES FOR SIMPLICITY

However not all Muslims shared this taste for the good life. As the empire grew some Muslims began to ask difficult questions: How should Muslims live? What kind of society were Muslims going to build out of their new empire? Was success in this world a proper concern for Muslims? What of the teachings of Muhammad and the Quran? For these Muslims material possessions and political power meant little if the deeper truths of the Quran and the teachings of Muhammad were ignored. Increasingly they turned away from the riches enjoyed by others around them to lead simple lives. They wore plain clothing and shunned the pursuit of money. Many saw poverty as a necessity. They dedicated themselves to the worship of God through meditation and prayer. In pursuing this way of life they became the first ascetics of Islam.

DEEP ATTACHMENT TO GOD

The models for these early ascetics were Muhammad and the first leaders of the community, men like Abu Bakr. Muhammad, they believed, had led a simple life of devotion to God. He had not permitted himself to be tempted by the luxuries of this world. After him Abu Bakr had also shunned wealth, preferring to live in a state of poverty and deep religious devotion. This was how the ascetics sought to lead their lives.

EARLY ASCETIC VOICES

One of the earliest voices of asceticism in Islam was that of al-Hasan al-Basri (d. 728). Theologian and teacher, al-Basri was famous for his powerful sermons. He is said to have warned his listeners that the world was a wretched place in which too many people had forgotten God. Stories circulated after his death of how he would spend long hours weeping, not only because of the state of the world but also out of fear of God's wrath on the day of judgment.

Not all the early ascetics were as gloomy; others thought of God with a profound sense of love. Rabia al-Adawiyya (d. 801) was one such individual. Like al-Basri she lived a simple life, shunning fine clothes and property. However her approach to the worship of God was very different. She described God in joyful language. It was as if she were describing the emotions of a human being in love, although for al-Adawiyya this was a far greater love. It is believed that she received during her lifetime many marriage proposals from men of her community and that she said no to each of them, claiming that her love was reserved for God.

For these devout early Muslims the greatest concern was God, whom they believed to be not only the creator of the universe but also the object of profound devotion and love. In different ways the ascetics expressed this deep attachment to God.

THE RISE OF SUFISM

Al-Basri, al-Adawiyya, and others like them attracted followers who shared their ideas and came to learn from them. These individuals in turn attracted students of their own, and in this way the ideas of asceticism and absolute devotion to God spread through the Islamic community.

These ideas and practices gave birth to Islamic mysticism, which is known as Sufism. The mystics, or Sufis, followed in the footsteps of the early ascetics but they may also have absorbed the teachings of Christian and Jewish mystics living in areas of the Middle East. For several generations they developed their ideas into more formal practices. It is important to note that Sufism is not a sect of Islam; it has been and still is practiced by both the Sunnis and Shia.

For the Sufis nothing was more important than the presence of God in the world. The Sufis saw life as a kind of journey in which one was constantly seeking a direct experience of God. Many of them believed that the way to seek that experience was to study the Quran and the hadith and to pray regularly—in short, to live the simple and disciplined life of a devout Muslim. Other Sufis disagreed, however. They felt that although prayer, the study of the Quran, and other duties of Muslims were necessary to a religious life, these practices were not enough. They sought a more direct and emotional experience of God through detachment from worldly affairs and through practices such as chanting or whirling which bring about a trance like state drawing the Sufi closer to being one with God.

At first the number of Sufis was very small. Usually they were scholars who spent their days in private discussing the nature of the spiritual life and the various ritual practices that could bring one closer to God. Their ideas were beyond the understanding of the average person and thus in the beginning had little popular appeal. Gradually, however, as the Sufis began to attract students and followers these mystics and holy men and holy women began to be seen as people with unusual spiritual powers.

As the ideas and ritual practices developed by the Sufis spread, informal study groups gathered in mosques or homes. By the start of the 10th century Sufi centers were established in which a Sufi master would serve as teacher and leader to followers. Some of these followers would go on to become teachers themselves, and many of their students would do the same in their turn. Thus Sufism was passed on from generation to generation.

By the 12th century Sufi centers could be found in cities, towns, and many rural areas throughout the Middle East and North Africa. These centers often included schools, mosques, and hostels where students could find a meal and a place to sleep. The heart of these centers was the house of the Sufi master, or shaykh. There the shaykh would conduct classes and lead followers through ritual practices.

SUFISM

The term *Sufism* probably comes from the Arabic word for wool, *suf.* It is thought that the early Muslim ascetics wore garments made from rough wool. These plain, unfinished garments were meant to symbolize the rejection of the luxuries and concerns of this world. The Muslim ascetics—those who are self-denying and live a very simple life for religious reasons—may have copied this practice from Christian monks living in the Middle East when Islam spread through the region.

THE SUFI ORDERS

By the 12th century the casual gatherings of the earlier period had evolved into formal organizations called Sufi orders. Each Sufi order, or *tariqa,* was built on the teachings of an early master and the students of that person. Their ideas and the rituals they used became formalized into specific forms of worship. Often the Sufi order would bear the name of its founder—usually the original master or an early student.

One of the earliest of the Sufi orders was the Qadiriya, named after Abd ai-Qadir

The Mausoleum of Mevlana Celaleddin Rumi in Konya, Turkey. Mevlana was a teacher and philosopher in the Sufi tradition. Born in 1207 he taught a doctrine of tolerance, charity, and awareness through love. After he died in 1273 a shrine was erected over his burial place. The mausoleum and its surrounding halls and living quarters have continued to attract large numbers of pilgrims over the centuries who feel that the spiritual power of this saint is still present.

al-Jilani (d. 1166). Of Iranian descent, Abd al-Qadir had been a legal scholar in Baghdad for many years. Only late in life did he begin to teach his Sufi ideas in public. His following quickly grew and a center was opened for him. Following his death his closest students continued to teach his ideas and open Qadiriya centers throughout the Middle East.

Other orders were established during the 12th and 13th centuries. The Suhrawardiya order, for example, took its name from

Umar ibn Abd Allah al-Suhrawardi (d. 1234), a religious scholar from the small Iranian town of Suhraward. Centers of this order were set up throughout Iran, Central Asia, and India.

Another example of Sufi orders, the Shadhiliya, was founded in North Africa by Ahmad ibn Abd Allah al-Shadhili (d. 1258). Born in Morocco and educated in Egypt, he attracted a large following in Egypt and later in Tunis, where he died. Centers of his

Graves of relatives of Salim Chishti at his mausoleum at Fatehpur Sikri, India. Salim Chishti was a highly respected Sufi who taught generosity to others through sharing of food and wealth, tolerance, respect for religious difference, and renunciation of material goods. He said the highest form of devotion was human service through helping those in misery or distress. In Islam saintly individuals are considered to have God-given spiritual power and visits to their tombs enable ordinary people to be touched by the saint's power.

order were soon present from Syria and Arabia across North Africa to Morocco.

By the 14th and 15th centuries Sufi orders were so widespread that they had considerable political power. Frequently governments in different regions of the Islamic world worked to win the support of the Sufi orders. The Safavid dynasty—which combined Sufism and radical Shii ideas and ruled Iran from the late-15th to the early-18th century—began as a Sufi movement.

Sufi orders played an important part in spreading Islam to new regions of the world. In India and areas of Central Asia, Malaysia, and Indonesia, plus large parts of sub-Saharan Africa, Sufi missionaries converted numerous people to Islam. Sufis accompanied merchants as they plied their trade across the Indian Ocean to various regions of Asia and across the trade routes of the African continent. They even marched with armies of various Islamic dynasties that widened the area of their control through conquest. In each region Sufi orders would set up centers where they would spread the message of Islam.

CHAPTER 6

MUSLIM RITUAL LIFE

Ritual is the means by which believers express in an orderly and regular way the deep beliefs that shape their lives. The most important of the ritual practices performed by Muslims are often called the Five Pillars of Islam. The first of these is *salat,* or daily prayer. Muslims carry out the *salat* five times daily. Each session of prayer begins with the call or summons to worship.

PRAYER AND SHAHADA

For many non-Muslims who travel to the Islamic world the call to prayer is one of the first clues that the daily lives of Muslims are different from their own. In Christian communities on Sunday mornings and on holidays the faithful are called to worship by the ringing of church bells. In the Islamic world it is the human voice that summons the believers every day.

ADHAN AND MUEZZIN

The call to prayer, or *adhan,* is made from the tall towerlike structure that is part of most mosques, called a *madhana,* or, in English, minaret. The individuals who call Muslims to prayer are known

Muslims at prayer in the courtyard of a mosque in Cairo, Egypt. Muslims say prayers, *salat,* five times daily in the direction of Mecca.

THE CALL TO PRAYER

The call to prayer is rather short. In its opening phrase, *Allahu akbar* (God is most great), it proclaims the important Islamic belief: God is the supreme being over all things. The call continues: "I bear witness that there is no deity except God," affirming the oneness of God, a central Islamic tenet. The phrase that follows names Muhammad as the prophet of Islam: "I bear witness that Muhammad is the messenger of God." Finally, in two phrases Muslims are told to "come to prayer" and "come to salvation." The idea behind these is that through prayer Muslims will worship God and in return be shown God's favor. The call to prayer ends as it began, with the phrase *"Allahu akbar."*

as *muadhdhins*. Traditionally the *muadhdhins*, or muezzins, made the call from the minaret itself using only their voices. Today it is common for these men to use microphones along with loudspeakers attached to the upper part of the minaret.

The muezzins deliver the call five times daily in a slow chant. In large towns and cities these voices form a long wave of sound. For the person visiting the Islamic world for the first time hearing the call can be a surprising and moving experience.

READY FOR PRAYER

After the *wudu* or ritual cleansing is complete the Muslim is ready for prayer. Although it is considered best to pray with other Muslims, it is perfectly acceptable to pray alone—at home, for example. When Muslims pray together they do so in a row, side by side. If men and women are together the women must pray behind or separately from the men. In many parts of the Islamic world women commonly pray at home, and it is the men who use the mosques regularly.

Standing in front of the rows of faithful is a single individual who leads the prayer. In the mosques the prayer is usually led by a person known as the imam, or prayer

Muslims prepare for each of the daily sessions of prayer with a short ritual of cleansing called the *wudu*. They wash with plain water at designated areas in the mosques. There are usually washbasins located in mosques for this purpose. At home or at the workplace Muslims simply use the facilities available.

leader. Outside the mosques when Muslims pray together they simply choose someone to lead; often this person is an older man chosen for his piety. The imam and the rows of persons behind him all face in the same direction, toward the holy city of Mecca and the sacred Kaaba.

PRAYER PHRASES AND POSITIONS

The *salat* consists of spoken phrases and a set of four postures: standing, bowing, prostrating, and sitting. These postures are carried out in a regular cycle that every Muslim learns as a child. There is a slightly different cycle of phrases and postures for each of the five daily prayers. It is considered a pious act for Muslims to repeat part or all of a cycle of prayer. The spoken phrases are short, voluntary prayers to God.

The prayer ends each time in the same way. Turning to the left and to the right each individual wishes the persons beside them peace and the blessings of God. This is one obvious way in which Muslims affirm that they are all members of the same community and that they share a common belief in the one God.

SHAHADA—BEARING WITNESS

The second of the pillars of Islam is a short statement known as the *shahada*, or bearing witness. The content of the *shahada* is similar to that of the call to prayer in that it proclaims the oneness of God: *There is no God but Allah and Muhammad is the messenger of Allah.* Most Muslims learn this statement when they are children. It is also the statement that all converts to Islam are required to make at the time of their conversion. This short utterance expresses the most fundamental beliefs of the Islamic faith, and learning and reciting it from the

THE FIVE PILLARS OF ISLAM

1. *salat*—prayer, carried out five times daily.

2. *shahada*—literally, "bearing witness"; a short statement affirming the greatness and oneness of Allah.

3. *sawm*—ritual fast that takes place each year during Ramadan, the ninth month of the Islamic calendar.

4. *zakat*—almsgiving; a religious tax set aside for the poor, the sick, the insane, and other less privileged groups of the Islamic community.

5. *hajj*—pilgrimage to the holy city, Mecca. The opportunity to perform the hajj occurs every year during the 12th Islamic month. Every Muslim is encouraged to participate at least once in his or her lifetime.

heart constitutes one's symbolic joining of the Islamic community.

FASTING AND THE ALMS

Sawm, or ritual fasting, is the third pillar of Islam. This fast takes place each year during Ramadan, the ninth month of the Islamic calendar. During the fast of Ramadan, which lasts for the entire month, strict restraints are placed upon the daily lives of Muslims. For example, they are not to eat or drink during the daylight hours. When the sun sets at the end of each day Muslims break the fast, but even then they are expected to eat and drink in moderation. The fast resumes the next morning.

Traditionally the beginning of the fast each day takes place when there is enough light in the sky to distinguish between a white and dark thread. Smoking is also forbidden during Ramadan, as are sexual relations. Ramadan is meant to be a time of physical abstinence and increased devotion to religious practice.

THE DEMANDS OF FASTING

The fast of Ramadan has been criticized by some Muslims because of the demands it makes upon the individual and upon society. Some Muslims argue that it is wasteful to have people observe the fast so rigorously. They insist that people naturally work more slowly and poorly when they are not eating. Some of these critics say that people should be given the choice of whether to fast or that the fast should be shortened in some way.

Against these arguments other Muslims respond that on the contrary the fast needs to be carefully observed because Ramadan is the only time when Muslims can fully concentrate on the practice of their faith while spending less time on the concerns of their everyday lives. It is a time of worship, contemplation, and for Muslims to strengthen their ties to family and community.

As is true in every religious community, there are many Muslims who do not closely observe the rituals of their faith. In private, for example, there are Muslims who choose not to fast, just as they often choose not to pray. What is interesting about Ramadan, however, is that in public it is extremely rare to find a Muslim eating or drinking during daylight hours. In many parts of the Islamic world cafés and restaurants remain closed through much of the day or only serve foreign tourists.

PRAYER AND CHARITY

For those who do observe the fast Ramadan is a spiritual time during which the Muslim concentrates more than ever on religious activities such as reading the Quran. It is not uncommon for Muslim men to reserve several days of Ramadan for spiritual retreat, when they turn away from the world and dedicate themselves to religious matters.

Ramadan is also a time when Muslims are expected to pay more attention to the hungry, the poor, and the deprived. Sharing food with less fortunate neighbors, for example, and donating clothes are ways in which this need is met. The Quran itself speaks of the support that Muslims should give to the needy in their communities. Such acts are also a way to demonstrate commitment to the faith.

The fourth pillar of Islam addresses the needs of the poor and the destitute more directly. The *zakat,* or almsgiving, is a kind of religious tax that all Muslims who can afford it are expected to pay at a specified time each year. The money collected is set aside for specific groups of people in the Islamic community including the poor, the sick, the mentally ill, and other groups who are unable to fend for themselves.

Muslims praying outside Regents Park Mosque in London at the end of Ramadan, when the festival of Id al-Fitr is celebrated. A box to collect the money given for *zakat* is beside the congregation.

For Muslims, the *zakat* is not considered charity but rather a religious obligation. In most of the Islamic world today the *zakat* is not enforced by the government. It is expected that Muslims will pay voluntarily. Like the other four pillars *zakat* plays an important part in the religious life of Muslims. The Quran states that giving alms is a duty that God requires of Muslims.

THE FIFTH PILLAR: PILGRIMAGE

The fifth pillar of Islam is one that all Muslims are strongly encouraged to perform at least once in their lives: the pilgrimage to the holy city of Mecca or, as it is called by Muslims, the hajj. Each year during the 12th Islamic month, Dhu al-Hijja, Muslims from all over the Islamic world perform the sacred journey. In Mecca they participate in an elaborate set of rituals during a period of five days. Unlike the other four pillars of Islam the hajj is not obligatory; only those who have reached maturity and who have the financial resources to pay for the trip while still providing for dependents at home are expected to perform the pilgrimage.

The first act of the pilgrimage is putting on a clean white garment known as an *ihram*. Wearing this garment is obligatory for men, but women are encouraged to wear the clothing that is native to their home countries. Women are required to keep their heads covered for the entire period of the pilgrimage, but men must keep their heads bare. From this point until the end of the hajj the pilgrims are considered to be in a state of holiness.

PERFORMING THE HAJJ RITUALS

After their arrival in Mecca pilgrims set out to perform the rituals of the hajj. Muslims from non-Arabic-speaking regions

A house in Egypt belonging to a Muslim who has gone on pilgrimage to Mecca. The house is painted with illustrations of Mecca and of the journey to Saudi Arabia to show neighbors that the pilgrimage is being made.

of the world are often assisted by guides known as *mutawwifs*, who are employees of the Saudi Arabian government. The guides translate for the pilgrims who do not speak or understand Arabic and assist them in carrying out the rituals.

Some of the rituals are performed at the choice of the individual. These include sessions of prayer and another ritual known as the *tawaf*, which involves walking around the Kaaba at least seven times. The pilgrims have less choice when it comes to the group rituals, which are the main rituals of the hajj.

The group rituals are carried out in a set order during the five days of the pilgrimage. One such ritual takes place in the small town of Mina just outside of Mecca. There, on a wide plain known as Arafat, pilgrims carry out the *wukuf*, or standing ceremony, in which they are required to be present on the plain from noon to sunset. It is the one occasion during the hajj when all the pilgrims must be together. Tents are erected for the huge crowd, and for this single day of the year the plain of Arafat resembles a very busy town. During these hours pilgrims are expected to pray quietly.

At the center of the plain is a small mountain known as the Mount of Mercy. During this day pilgrims ascend the mountain, where they ask God to forgive them for their sins. All pilgrims must carry out the full set of rituals at Arafat; failure to do so means the pilgrimage was incomplete and must be repeated in another year.

"VISITORS" OF GOD

Although the pilgrimage to Mecca may be a financial burden for some and especially strenuous for the elderly, most devout Muslims yearn to take part in it. For the individual Muslim the importance of the hajj cannot be overemphasized. In a way the pilgrimage is a greater version of the *salat*—the prayer for which Muslims each day face in the direction of Mecca and the Kaaba. During the pilgrimage, however, the Muslim is actually in Mecca, which is sometimes referred to as the house of God. Thus in Mecca the pilgrim is in a way one of God's visitors. As the house of God Mecca is the holiest site in the world for Muslims.

THE FAREWELL *TAWAF*

When the five days of the hajj are over the pilgrims take off the *ihram*. During the next few days pilgrims continue to pray and perform at least two more of the *tawafs* around the Kaaba. With the second of these, which is called the farewell *tawaf*, the pilgrimage is then considered complete. Many pilgrims add one last part to their voyage—a visit to Muhammad's tomb in Medina—so that they may pay their respects to the prophet of Islam.

The pilgrimage brings together Muslims from all over the world. It is a time when Muslims of many different backgrounds, speaking different languages, and practicing different customs share a common and intense experience. Ever since Muhammad set out on the first pilgrimage to Mecca many accounts of the hajj have been written. These descriptions show how moving the experience of the pilgrimage is for Muslims.

AFTER HAJJ

The pilgrims make their way back from Mecca to their home countries by plane, bus, ship, and train. Upon their arrival they are usually greeted with a joyous welcome by their families and neighbors. The accomplishment of the pilgrimage is a time to celebrate. The pilgrim, after all, has been through one of the most important events in the life of a Muslim. Having made the holy journey to Mecca and the Kaaba, the pilgrim is now a hajji or, if the pilgrim is a woman, a hajja.

THE RITUALS OF THE SHIA

While all Muslims are expected to carry out the hajj and the other four pillars of Islam to the best of their abilities, the Shia perform additional rituals as well. The focus of the most important of these rituals is the 10th day of the Islamic month of Muharram. On that day in 680 Husayn, the grandson of Muhammad, was killed in battle by Umayyad soldiers. The day is known as Ashura.

During Ashura, on stage, actors carry out the events of Husayn's death in remarkable detail. More than just his death is portrayed, however. All of the events involving the Shii community and its imams in their struggle against the Umayyad and Abbasid caliphs is described and acted out. The climax of the performance is the attack on Husayn and his infant son.

As the story builds to its inevitable climax emotions both on and off the stage begin to grow. Throughout the performance members of the audience offer advice to the actors, shout and laugh when the imams are doing well, and fall sad when things turn badly for the imams and their followers. These emotions reach a peak with the attack on Husayn. As the Umayyad soldiers close in with their spears and swords, hacking away at the imam and his horse, and when Husayn's head is finally severed, members of the audience weep and shout out curses against the Umayyad soldiers. On occasion, with a particularly vivid performance, audience members have been known to leap on stage and rush at the actors playing the soldiers in order to protect Husayn and his family.

TAAZIYA—THE PASSION PLAY

The centerpiece of the rituals of Ashura is the elaborate performance known as *taaziya*, or passion play. Performed during the Islamic month of Muharram in every Shii community, the passion play is a detailed and emotional reenactment of the death of Husayn. While it may be thought of as theater by westerners, it is quite unlike the plays one might attend in the West. One obvious difference is that audience participation is not only expected but encouraged.

ASHURA PROCESSIONS

Other ritual events surround the passion play. Frequently before the play a procession is held in which models of the Kaaba and the

Husayn, the grandson of Muhammad who was killed in battle by Umayyad soldiers in 680, is remembered during the day of Ashura. This is during the *rawza khavani,* or recital of the suffering of the Imam Husayn. An individual or family will invite a group of friends to a private gathering. There a professional reciter will tell the story of Husayn's martyrdom, often in great detail. A skilled reciter will touch his listeners deeply, bringing tears to their eyes and perhaps rousing them to their feet crying out the name of Husayn. Like the passion play these can be extremely emotional events.

tombs of the imams are carried. Members of the community display ornate banners drawn with scenes of the deaths of the imams and on which are written verses of the Quran and sayings from the imams.

The processions of the *taaziya* include another event that many non-Shiis have found disturbing. In the processions march lines of men, many stripped to the waist, striking themselves across the shoulders or head with knives and chains while chanting rhythmically the name of Husayn. For the foreign visitor these scenes can be shocking. For the Shia their meaning is clear: Ashura is a time to express deep emotions of pain and anger. In the year 680 the Shia had called on the Imam Husayn to claim his place as leader of the Islamic community. When he finally responded to their call and set out to meet them, they failed to support him. Rather than march out to join him in fighting the hated Umayyad rulers, the Shia stayed home and left Husayn to be slaughtered. It is during Ashura that the Shii community expresses guilt over its failure to act and anguish over the death of the beloved Husayn.

TOMBS OF THE IMAMS

The Shia honor the imams in other ways. In premodern times local dynasties could not always guarantee the safety of pilgrims traveling to Mecca. So for a long time visitations to the tombs of the imams were seen as an acceptable substitute to the hajj. Today, even though the Shia of Iran, Iraq, and other Shii areas take part in the pilgrimage to Mecca, it is considered a pious act to visit these tombs and as well as those of lesser members of the Alid family.

The Names of God

Among the 99 names of God are al-Rahman ("The Compassionate"), al-Rahim ("The Merciful"), al-Aziz ("The Mighty"), and al-Khaliq ("The Creator").

THE RITUALS OF THE SUFIS

Throughout Islamic history Sunnis and Shiis alike have also carried out the rituals of Sufism. By the 14th century Sufism was so widespread in the Islamic world that it was commonplace for ordinary Muslims to carry out Sufi rituals. The broad term used for these rituals is *dhikr*.

In carrying out *dhikr* the Sufi repeats the names of God—Muslims believe that God has 99 known names—and his attributes. *Dhikrs* may be carried out in private, where they are usually practiced to complement prayer, or they may be performed in groups by the Sufi orders. Each of these orders has its own special *dhikr* developed by the early masters of the order and their students hundreds of years ago.

Whirling dervishes in Turkey carrying out *dhikr* by revolving very fast and repeating the praises of God. These revolving movements create a spiritual state that brings the person involved closer to God.

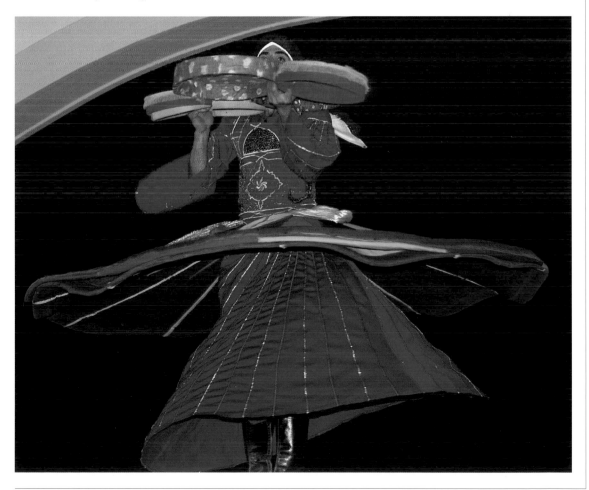

The broad term for Sufi rituals is *dhikr*. These rituals can be carried out in private or as a group. In the group *dhikrs* some of the orders simply repeat Allah (the Arabic word for God) over and over again, sometimes in a soft whisper, sometimes in a loud, clear chant. Some orders will do so while sitting calmly. Most prefer to stand and often the participants will sway from side to side as they utter the *dhikr*. Other Sufi orders have developed more elaborate rituals where long phrases in praise of God and Muhammad are repeated. Such rituals may include intense physical movement such as dancing or a strong rocking motion of the upper body. Regardless of the form it takes the goal of the *dhikr* is nearly always the same: to draw the person closer to God.

Performing *dhikr* became a common part of the religious lives of many, if not most, Muslims in the 14th century. In neighborhoods and villages throughout the Islamic world Muslims met in mosques and Sufi centers to perform *dhikr* with the other members of their orders. *Dhikr* would be performed on religious holidays and on other special occasions such as the prophet Muhammad's birthday.

POSSESSING *BARAKA*

By this period another kind of ritual practice was also common. For the ordinary Muslim the religious world was inhabited not only by God and the prophets but also by deeply spiritual individuals we might refer to as saints. Among these saints were Sufi masters, holy men and holy women who were seen in many parts of the Islamic world as possessing *baraka*—a spiritual power given them by God. *Baraka* enabled them to carry out miraculous acts such as healing the sick.

The *baraka* of the saintly individual was believed to live on after the individual's death. It was carried on by the members of the saint's family and more often it was believed to inhabit the tomb in which the saint was buried. Consequently visits to the tombs of saints became commonplace. For ordinary Muslims the goal of such a visit was to be touched by the saint's powers—by the *baraka*.

A visit to the tomb of a saintly individual often involved certain rituals. Visitors would bring small offerings to the saint or the saint's family. Plates of food, small gifts, or sums of money were common offerings. Visitors would also touch the tomb of the saint, which would become worn in places where it had been touched often over the years. Prayers might also be performed or a portion of the Quran read aloud. For example in visits by Muslims to the tomb of a local saint in the southern Moroccan city of Marrakech, after reciting a brief Quranic verse or prayer the visitors then leave small rags tied to the bars crisscrossing the windows of the tomb. In this way the visitors seek to win the help of the saint and a small touch of the *baraka*.

OPPOSITION TO VENERATION OF SAINTS— THE WAHHABI MOVEMENT

Many in the community, especially religious leaders, scholars, and better-educated Muslims, have objected strongly to the veneration of the saints. In their view the teachings of Islam are corrupted by such practices. Their opinions seem to have led a number of Muslims to stop engaging in these activities, but even today others continue to practice them.

One particularly angry attack on the practice of tomb visits, and on Sufism as a whole, came from a radical movement that appeared in Arabia in the 18th century. Known as the Wahhabi movement, it was able to seize control of much of the Arabian Peninsula in the early 20th century. The state it established bore the name of a large tribal clan that supported the movement: the Saud clan. This was the creation of what we know today as Saudi Arabia. One of the first measures taken by the new state was the destruction of the tombs of the Sufi masters and the other saints. The veneration of the saints was denounced. As a result today Saudi Arabia is one of the few areas of the Islamic world where Sufism is completely absent.

CHAPTER 7

THE PATTERNS OF ISLAMIC LIFE

Although many other customs and habits are common throughout the Islamic world, it would be wrong to think that all Muslims live in the same way. Muslim lives are shaped not only by Islamic norms and activities but also by the customs and habits that are native to each area of the Islamic world. For this reason Muslims in Indonesia or Senegal do not live in exactly the same way that Muslims in China, Afghanistan, or Morocco do. Everywhere Muslims have adapted Islamic norms and values to local customs and beliefs.

The variety of languages that Muslims speak is an example of the important differences among Muslims. Arabic, as the language of the Quran, has a special status among Muslims and is almost always used when the Quran is recited. Scholars and students of Islam throughout the world strive to learn to read and write Arabic; many come to Egypt's al-Azhar and other universities in Arab countries to do so. The vast majority of Muslims, however, speak no Arabic other than a handful of verses from the Quran. In Pakistan Urdu is the common language of Muslims; in

A Muslim congregation praying at al-Faisal mosque, Pakistan. Islamic prayer, or *salat,* consists of a cycle of postures including prostration. At the close of each session of prayer worshippers turn to the left and right to wish peace and the blessings of God upon those worshipping beside them.

Muslims gathered for Friday prayers in the streets outside a mosque in Abu Dhabi. Unlike Sunday in the Christian world, Friday is not considered an official day of rest by Muslims. Still it has become traditional in many Islamic countries for businesses to close around noon so that business owners and employees may attend the Friday prayer.

Turkey and parts of Central Asia it is Turkish; and in Iran Farsi is spoken on a daily basis. Other languages are spoken in other regions of the Islamic world. This does not mean, however, that the Quran cannot be understood by these Muslims. In each non-Arabic-speaking region local languages are used in religion classes and in sermons to teach the Quran and hadith. The Quran is also made available in translation or, as they are known in Islam, interpretations, as it is believed to be impossible to exactly translate the Quran.

Although their way of life may vary greatly from region to region and country to country, depending on local customs and habits, most Muslims have some patterns of life in common.

THE FRIDAY PRAYER

In Islam Friday is the one day of the week set aside for special religious observances. Every Friday Muslims attend a special session of worship that takes place at noon. In many areas of the Islamic world mosques are so crowded on Fridays that people pray outside on long mats provided by the mosques. In Cairo, for example, it is not unusual to find some side streets closed to traffic on Friday mornings. Long straw mats are rolled out on these streets to accommodate the faithful.

KHUTBA—RECITATION AND SERMON

What makes the Friday prayer session special is the sermon given by the imam or by another individual chosen for their knowledge of the Quran. The sermon is known as the *khutba* and it is made up of two parts: The preacher begins with a recitation of a portion of the Quran and then proceeds to the sermon. Most often the subject of the sermon is the Quranic passage itself. The preacher will explain the passage in simple language and discuss how that portion of the sacred book relates to the lives of his listeners. During the month of Ramadan, for example, the preacher will discuss how fasting is an important duty required of the Muslim.

RELIGION, POLITICS, AND SOCIAL ISSUES

While most often the preacher will address religious matters, he may use the Friday sermon to talk of other subjects as well. For example he may comment on social problems such as poverty, crime, and drug abuse; in times of war he may urge his listeners to support the government against its enemies, or he may call on the government to find a peaceful solution. In many parts of the Islamic world the Friday sermon given by a leading preacher will be broadcast over the radio or be shown on television, reaching millions of people.

THE MOSQUES

Not all mosques are used for the Friday sermon. Most mosques are fairly small and are generally used by residents of the immediate neighborhood. The small local mosque is known as a *masjid*, or place of prostration. For the Friday prayer session a larger and

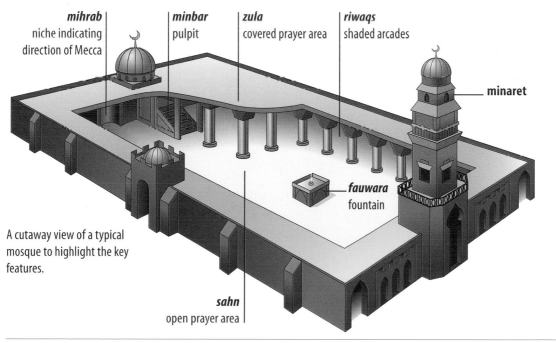

mihrab
niche indicating direction of Mecca

minbar
pulpit

zula
covered prayer area

riwaqs
shaded arcades

minaret

fauwara
fountain

A cutaway view of a typical mosque to highlight the key features.

sahn
open prayer area

more centrally located mosque, or *jami,* is used. In small towns and villages only one such mosque might exist, whereas in the larger cities a small number of these larger mosques are present in different areas of the city.

All mosques whether small or large have certain similar features. Most if not all provide running water so that those coming to pray can carry out the *wudu,* or ritual cleansing, that is expected of all Muslims before prayer. All have large, clear central areas where those in prayer can line up in rows for the performance of worship. And all have what is known as the *mihrab.* Muslims must pray in the direction of Mecca and in order to indicate the direction of the holy city a niche is built into the appropriate wall. This niche is the *mihrab,* while the direction of Mecca is known as the *qibla.* The Quran itself calls on Muslims to "turn their faces" in the direction of Mecca and the Kaaba in prayer.

AL-AZHAR UNIVERSITY, CAIRO

Over the course of Islamic history several of these large Friday mosques became important educational centers. Perhaps the most renowned of all is the university of al-Azhar in the historical center of Cairo. For centuries it has attracted students and scholars from all parts of the Islamic world: Students from the Sudan or Nigeria interact with those from as far away as Malaysia and Pakistan. For much of its history al-Azhar was strictly a religious center where Muslims could study the Quran and hadith (the accounts of Muhammad's teachings) and delve into other areas of Islamic education. Today al-Azhar is a major university offering courses in a range of fields in addition to the religious subjects it has traditionally offered.

Many mosques also have a *minbar*—the pulpit from which the preacher gives the Friday sermon. In some mosques the *minbar* may only be a raised platform, whereas in many others it has a set of stairs leading to a small stage closed in by a railing. It can be quite an elaborate structure. In the mosque of Ibn Tulun in Cairo, one of the oldest mosques in the world, the *minbar* is built of dark brown wooden panels carved in wonderful and very intricate designs.

ANNUAL FESTIVALS

The larger mosques such as al-Azhar are commonly located in busy commercial areas. From Islam's early history merchants have been drawn to the mosques because they are centers of so much activity, religious and otherwise. As a result one finds in Islamic cities large numbers of shops, bookstores, and small restaurants lining the streets and alleys that circle these mosques. With mosque and marketplace side by side these areas are usually among the busiest and most congested parts of town. They become especially crowded during religious holidays and other special occasions such as the month-long fast of Ramadan.

RAMADAN

Although Ramadan is considered a duty that Muslims are expected to take quite seriously and the physical demands of the fast are taxing, Ramadan also has its lighter side. In most parts of the Islamic world it brings a marked change in the pace of life. Activity during the daylight hours slows considerably; people become quieter, less active, and sometimes more calm than they normally are. With the end of the day, however, the fast is broken, and it is expected that Muslims will break the fast with prayer and a short meal known as the *iftar*. In some parts of the Islamic world, such as Morocco, the meal may consist of a thick soup with bread and fruit.

Following the breaking of the fast things grow festive. In the towns and cities of the Middle East, as well as other areas of the Islamic world, it is customary for Muslims to go out after the *iftar*. They visit with family and friends or simply stroll. Shopping districts often remain quite busy as shops and restaurants stay open. In Cairo, near the al-Azhar mosque, a book fair is held during Ramadan. And nearby, beneath large canvas tents, members of Sufi groups recite the Quran and perform their *dhikrs*.

The high point of Ramadan comes toward the end of the month. On the evening of the 27th day Muslims celebrate what is known as the Night of Power. According to Islamic tradition it was on this night in 610 that Muhammad first received the revelation of the Quran. In many parts of the Muslim world the evening is a noisy one as young men let off fireworks in the streets.

CALLIGRAPHY

Christian churches are usually decorated with stained glass, paintings, and statues, but mosques very rarely are. Instead they are decorated with inscriptions of the Quran. These can cover the walls and ceilings of the mosque, including the inside of the dome that sits atop many mosques. These inscriptions are an example of the dominant art form in Islamic culture, calligraphy, and arise from a ban on depicting any living creature, Muhammad, or Allah.

ID AL-FITR

Another important occasion comes with the end of Ramadan. On the first day of the next month, Shawwal, Muslims celebrate a special and long-awaited holiday known as the Feast of Fast Breaking, or Id al-Fitr. For three days Muslims gather with family and friends for long meals, the sharing of gifts, and often religious devotion. In many Islamic countries, the Id is a national holiday. Those who are abroad for work or study travel home to be with family. For many Muslims it is a time to celebrate the renewed commitment to their faith and to offer thanks to God for having seen them through the long fast.

ID AL-ADHA

Another important celebration of the year comes during the month of pilgrimage, Dhu al-Hijja. One of the rituals carried out toward the end of the pilgrimage in Mecca is the sacrifice of animals, usually sheep, goats, or camels. In Mecca, while some of

Muslims praying at a mosque on the island of Phuket in Thailand. Before entering the mosque Muslims remove their shoes, placing them in a designated area near the entrance. Mosques range greatly in size from the enormous "communal" mosques found in many urban centers to those much smaller in size found in villages and local neighborhoods.

the meat is eaten by the pilgrims, much of it is distributed to the poor. In the rest of the Islamic world a similar sacrifice is made by each household or neighborhood.

In the weeks leading up to this celebration, known as Id al-Adha, or the Feast of Sacrifice, in city centers as well as in suburbs it is quite common to see great numbers of sheep and goats, sometimes in unexpected places. At times one sees adult sheep being transported in the back seats of taxis, tied in bundles on top of buses, and feeding on the terraces of apartment buildings and in the back rooms of shops.

ISLAMIC DAYS OF OBSERVANCE

Id al-Adha (known also as **Id al-Kabir**)—This is the festival of sacrifice held throughout the Islamic world on the 10th day of the month of Dhu al-Hijja. The sacrifice is an important element of the pilgrimage to Mecca, the hajj.

Id al-Fitr (known also as **Id al-Saghir**)—Held on the first day of the month of Shawwal, this is the feast celebrating the end of Ramadan. This is a particularly joyful event for Muslims.

Mawlid al-Nabi—The birthday of the prophet Muhammad, held on the 12th day of the month of Rabia I. A particularly popular event. Nabi, or "prophet," is one of the titles given to Muhammad. The Shia celebrate his birthday on the 17th day of that month, which is also the birthday of Jafar al-Sadiq, the Sixth Imam.

Ashura—During the first 10 days of the month of Muharram the Shii community commemorates the suffering and death of Imam Husayn, the prophet's grandson and the Third Imam. These events reach their peak on the 10th day, which is known as Ashura.

The Shia also commemorate the birthdays of each of the imams. In Iran, which has a Twelver Shii majority, each of these 12 birthdays is considered a national holiday. For example the first of their imams, Ali ibn Abi Talib, is believed to have been born on the 13th day of the month of Rajab.

Muslim children in Lahore, Pakistan, dressed in new clothes
to celebrate Id al-Fitr, marking the end of the month of
Ramadan. This is often a national holiday in Muslim countries
as family meet to pray, share feasts, and exchange gifts.

MAWLIDS

For many Muslims, though certainly not all, the *mawlid* is another occasion of celebration. It is a festival marking the birthday of a saint or some other revered person of the past. No *mawlid* is more widely observed than that of Muhammad. Known as the Mawlid al-Nabi and held every year during Rabia al-Awwal, the third Islamic month, it signals the deep veneration felt by Muslims for Muhammad.

The Mawlid al-Nabi is celebrated in a variety of ways. Special prayers are said in Muhammad's honor, for example, and often Sufi groups will hold public *dhikrs* in which his name is praised. In large cities and towns centrally located areas are decorated with hanging lights and banners, giving a festive atmosphere.

Musims

The calendar year is marked by *mawlids* or celebrations, most often held in honor of saints. These celebrations, known in some areas as *musims*, can vary in size and importance. A saint may be venerated in only a particular town or even a neighborhood, in which case the festival is attended by a limited number of people. Other *mawlids* however can attract Muslims, not to mention tourists, from all over a particular nation or even region of the Islamic world.

FESTIVAL OF MULAY IDRIS, MOROCCO

In Morocco the site of one annual celebration in honor of a saint is the small town of Mulay Idris. Located near the northern city of Meknes, the town features an elaborate shrine in which is located the tomb of Mulay Idris, after whom the town is named. Sometimes referred to as the national saint of Morocco, Mulay Idris was the founder of the first Islamic dynasty in Morocco in the late eighth century. Topped by a beautiful green dome, the shrine was built in the latter part of the 15th century. Since that time the festival in honor of Mulay Idris has drawn large numbers of people from all over Morocco and remains a popular event to the present day.

CELEBRATIONS FOR AL-BADAWI, EGYPT

In sheer numbers perhaps no *mawlid* is larger than that of Ahmad al-Badawi, held each fall in the Egyptian town of Tanta. It is an enormously popular event—one that many Egyptians are reluctant to miss. The celebrations in Mulay Idris and for al-Badawi in Tanta share a number of features. At both events people gather to be touched by the *baraka* of the saint. Those who can try to touch the tomb of the saint while murmuring prayers or repeating the name of Mulay Idris or al-Badawi. In the *baraka,* it is believed, lies the power to bring good luck, strength, good health, or even success in school or in a business deal.

MUSICIANS, STORYTELLERS, AND PREACHERS

These celebrations are usually very festive. Sufi groups gather to hold their *dhikrs* and attract new members. Processions take place organized by Sufis and other groups as well. During these processions banners are displayed and often the leader of the Sufi order is brought out on horseback for all to see. Attracted by the large crowds musicians, storytellers, traveling merchants, and preachers come to practice their skills and earn money. Tents in which are sold everything from food to clothes to spices and charms are erected in any clear area. Both events last for days and many of those in attendance spend nights wherever they can—be it in a mosque, on the floors of houses and shops, or in a quiet area on the ground.

Feast days, *mawlids,* and other such occasions are celebrated throughout the Islamic world. If one turns from these noisier, more public events to the quieter world of Muslim family life, one discovers patterns that are much more private but no less a part of the lives of Muslims the world over.

MUSLIM CHILDHOOD

Several events mark the first years of a Muslim child's life. Around the time of birth the infant is given a Muslim name. It is common, at least within devout Muslim families, to use the names of highly revered figures of Islamic history.

Muhammad is, as one might expect, the most popular name of all for male children. Others include Umar, after one of the first caliphs, and Ali, after Ali ibn Abi Talib. The names Hasan and Husayn are popular as well since these were the names of

Muhammad's grandsons—both of whom it is believed he loved dearly. Since they were also the first of the imams their names are particularly popular among the Shia. Often males are also given names that are formed from one of the names of God, such as Abd Allah (servant of God) or Abd al-Rahman (servant of the All-Merciful).

Female children similarly are named after Muhammad's wives and other important and well-known women in early Islamic history. Khadija, the name of Muhammad's first wife; Fatima, the name of one of his daughters; and Aisha, the name of another of Muhammad's wives, are all popular names.

A Muslim teacher helps children in their kindergarten class at the Al-Ghazaly Muslim elementary school in Jersey City, New Jersey, one of 10 such schools in the state.

RECITING QURANIC VERSES

The Quran is where formal education begins for many Muslim children. In the first year of school or in a small center known as a *kuttab* children learn to read by reciting verses from the Quran. In this way they learn not only to read but also to recognize the central teachings of their faith. One of the first parts of the Quran learned by all Muslim children is the first sura: the Surat al-Fatiha.

MALE CIRCUMCISION

For Muslim boys an event that happens early in their lives is circumcision, or cutting away of the male foreskin. In some Muslim areas, this takes place around the age of 10. In other areas it is not the age that matters, but when the boy is able to recite the entire Quran aloud for the first time. Although the operation itself is usually over in minutes, the occasion is often celebrated in various ways. In parts of Morocco, for example, it is customary for those families that can afford to rent a horse to have the boy paraded around the neighborhood on horseback.

FEMALE CIRCUMCISION

In some parts of the Muslim world, girls and young women may undergo a ritual called female circumcision, or clitoridectomy. This operation, which ranges in degree from a small incision to the removal of the clitoris, is carried out in parts of Africa. Some Muslims there consider this ritual necessary to preserve the girl's purity and to make her marriageable, believing it to be a religious duty. The operation can have serious health consequences for the young woman, which may include death either at the time of the surgery or later in childbirth.

In recent years female circumcision has been banned in Egypt and there is pressure from world health organizations on other governments of the area to follow Egypt's example. Many Islamic scholars find that the practice has no basis in the Quran but has come into Islam from pre-Islamic customs. However it remains a deeply rooted practice that will take many years of education to change.

MARRIAGE

Muslims are encouraged to marry and to bear children. In many parts of the Islamic world, as in the non-Islamic world, it has been customary for marriages to be arranged by parents or guardians. This practice is changing; in urban areas, and among the educated classes, a young woman commonly has at least a say in whom she marries. Young men and women may see each other in university classes or at family gatherings but dating remains rare in the Islamic world. In many regions for an unmarried couple to be seen together in public alone is still considered behavior that brings shame on both of their families.

UNITING TWO FAMILIES

Marriage between two people, according to Islamic law, is settled with a contract in which the rights and duties of both the man and woman arc laid out and agreed on by both persons. In many parts of the Islamic world marriage is seen as the uniting of two families rather than just two individuals. Most often the ceremony itself is rather simple and quiet.

However for the celebrations that follow families often spend large sums of money on food, clothes, and gifts. The lavishness of the celebrations depends on the wealth of the families involved, and even the poorest families will borrow money in order to stage what they believe will be considered a proper wedding. Usually these will be held in the home or just outside the home of one of the two families. The celebrations can last throughout the night or even longer. They are often community events in which an entire village or neighborhood will be invited to join in the celebration. Very often men and women celebrate at the same time but in separate buildings or areas.

MARRIAGE TO MORE THAN ONE WIFE

An issue that has been discussed a great deal within the Islamic community is whether men should marry more than one woman. (This practice is known as polygyny in which a man has more than one wife.) Polygyny seems to have been present in pre-Islamic Arabia, and it is known that Muhammad himself had a number of wives by the end of his life. The Quran states that men may marry up to four wives but only if they can treat each of them equally and fairly (4.3).

Since the rise of Islam polygyny has been a standard practice, but scholars are uncertain as to how widespread it has been. Today the practice is the subject of much argument. There are those who say that the practice should be banned because it is impossible to treat more than one wife equally. Many Muslims—both men and women—argue that it is also a form of great dis-

Male family members and friends gathered during wedding celebrations to sign a marriage contract in Tripoli, Libya. The marriage contract is a legal document that outlines the duties of the husband and wife and it is often regarded as the uniting of two families.

crimination against women and so should be abolished. They point to another verse in the Quran: "You will not be able to treat your wives equally, no matter how hard you try."

FOOD AND DRINK

In addition to a discussion of marriage the Quran provides guidelines for other aspects of the Muslim's personal life, including eating and drinking habits. Muslims are forbidden to consume certain kinds of food and drink. Pork for example is forbidden, as is the eating of any meat from an animal that has died of natural causes. Muslims may only eat from an animal that has been slaughtered properly, which means that its blood has been drained as much as possible after the slaughter. The drinking of alcohol is also strictly forbidden. The Quran mentions wine specifically, but it is believed that this really meant all substances containing alcohol. This includes cooking wine and for many Muslims the ban includes any medicines that have alcohol in them.

In many countries of the Islamic world, however, alcoholic beverages are sold and consumed. Some of these countries, such as Algeria, Morocco, and Egypt, have their own national beer and wine companies. In bars and restaurants beer and wine are sold, although usually only non-Muslim tourists order such drinks. The presence and use of these substances has created a great deal of debate in which devout Muslims and religious leaders have called for the banning of the sale and manufacture of all alcoholic beverages. On occasion bars and hotels have been raided by Muslim activists who proceed to smash bottles of alcohol and even burn bars to the ground. In some urban areas—Cairo and Casablanca for example—alcoholism has been recognized as a social problem.

DEATH

As in every faith death is marked in Islam with solemn rituals. The last hours of a dying Muslim's life are passed with a recitation of the Quran. The 36th sura of the Quran, entitled Ya Sin, is concerned with death and God's judgment, so it is considered

REMINDER OF GOD'S POWER

The last three verses of Ya Sin, the 36th sura of the Quran, remind the listener of God's power at the end of life:

Is not He, who created the heavens and earth, able to create the like of them? Yes, surely, He is the Creator and the All-Knowing. His command, when He desires a thing, is to say to it: "Be!," and it is.
So glory to Him in whose hand is power over everything. Unto Him you shall be returned.

—36.81–83

the most appropriate part of the Quran to read. A family member or the local imam recites this sura out loud both to comfort the dying person and to prepare that person for the coming judgment.

Following the person's death a prescribed set of rituals is performed. The body is first carefully washed and prepared for burial by being wrapped in a clean white cloth. Then a funeral service is performed, sometimes in a mosque, often simply at home. The service is usually led by the local imam. Following this service the body is then taken to the grave site. It is not required for the corpse to be placed

Gravestones in a Muslim cemetery.

in a coffin. Muslims do not spend a great deal of money on either the burial preparations or the burial itself. The deceased is buried quickly, usually the morning following the death.

The body, either in a casket or simply upon a funeral bier (a stand on which a corpse or coffin is placed), is then carried in a procession of family and friends to the burial site. The procession for a well-known individual will draw large numbers of people, many of whom may join along the way to the graveyard. In 1970 Cairo in Egypt was the scene of probably the largest single funeral procession in history. Jamal Abd al-Nasir, perhaps the greatest and most respected Arab leader of the 20th century, died of a heart attack in September of that year. His funeral is said to have attracted more than four million people, not only from Egypt but also from across the Arabic-speaking world and beyond.

> ## FINAL RECITATION AT THE GRAVESIDE
>
> Like the funeral service, a Muslim's burial site is very simple. When the body is placed in the ground, care is taken to see that the head is facing in the direction of Mecca. If the body is in a coffin, usually it is marked to indicate the place of the head. Pious words are then said over the grave and then there is a recitation of the Surat al-Fatiha, the first sura, or chapter, of the Quran. The recitation of this sura symbolizes that the life that has just ended was that of a Muslim. Because Muslims learn the sura early in life, often as one of their first lessons in school, and use it frequently over the course of their lives on all sorts of occasions, it is fitting that at the end of their lives the sura is recited for them this last time.

CHAPTER 8

ISLAM AND THE MODERN WORLD

By the 18th century the Islamic community had changed considerably from those first years in Medina, when a small group of Muslims joined Muhammad in establishing the first Islamic settlement. With the number of Muslims now in the millions the community stretched from the Atlantic coast of Morocco to the many islands of Indonesia. Islam had truly become a world religion.

For 200 years three empires—Mughal, Safavid, and Ottoman—had controlled much of the Islamic world. With their centralized forms of government and strong armies they had brought stability to the lands of Islam. With stability had also come trade, which meant greater prosperity for all three empires. However all of this came to an end as political and economic strength gave way to decline. The Safavids fell from power in the 18th century and then the Mughal dynasty crumbled in the 19th century.

The Turkish Ottoman empire seemed to survive but the declaration of Serbia's autonomy (self-rule) in 1829, Greece's revolt in 1830, and Lebanon's independence in 1861 were sure signs of its declining power. Turkey, after the Crimean War in 1856, also lost

A Muslim family walking in a San Francisco park. The highest concentrations of Muslims in the United States are in California, New York, Michigan, and Illinois.

the Balkans. So even though the Ottoman Empire would survive into the 20th century its strength was greatly diminished.

THE CHALLENGE OF THE FUTURE

As the Safavid, Mughal, and Ottoman empires crumbled the Islamic world faced an uncertain future. In the age of the strongly unified empires the Islamic religion was viewed as the source of the empires' unity. In the newly autonomous Greece, Lebanon, Serbia, and the weakened Turkey the concern for survival made people ask why the Islamic world has suffered this collapse.

Many religious Muslims wanted to remove the additions that in their view had divided the religion and split its followers into disagreeing competitive groups. They wanted to rid Islam of such Sufi practices as the worship of saints and the inclusion of music and dancing in rituals. Many of these critics sensed that the Sufi saints themselves had become competitors to Allah and they called for the suppression or reform of the Sufi orders. Other religious-minded people blamed religious scholars, or ulama, for mechanically repeating earlier legal decisions in a way that deadened Islamic life. They wanted their scholars to recapture the original spirit of Islam and apply its basic beliefs to the challenges of a new age. Only wide and deep religious reform, these people believed, would bring fruitful guidance and support for building modern Islamic nations.

A NEW ISLAM

The new reformers argued that the time had come to put Islam and Islamic society back on the right path. This meant ridding Islam of non-Islamic practices, following the duties and regulations of the sharia more closely, and dealing with the new problems of society in creative ways.

For many of these Muslims the model of action was Muhammad, whom they felt had reformed the society of his day. They sought to follow his example by bringing change to their own societies so that Muslims could face the challenges of the modern world with energy and creativity.

THE EMERGENCE OF SAUDI ARABIA

Reform movements appeared in different areas of the Islamic world during the 18th and 19th centuries. Perhaps the earliest was the Wahhabi movement begun by Ibn al-Wahhab (d. 1792), a conservative preacher who had studied law and theology in Mecca and Damascus in the middle of the 18th century. He saw the threat to Islam as coming from within, not from the West. The chief internal causes for the corruption of Islam he judged to be Sufism and worship of the saints. He argued fiercely that Muslims should seek guidance only from the Quran and hadith. He reminded people of the model given by Muhammad for the true Islamic way of life that modern Muslims had forgotten.

A Bedouin girl in the Sahara Desert. Islam is the majority religion throughout north Africa.

The Wahhabi movement gained the attention and support of an Arabian tribal leader named Ibn Saud. With the help of the tribe's fighters the movement by 1803 dominated much of the Arabian Peninsula, including Mecca. In Mecca and Medina the followers of Wahhab destroyed Sufi centers and the tombs of saints. They even desecrated the tomb of Muhammad and his closest followers to prevent anyone from visiting them in a search for miracles. Although the Wahhabi state was destroyed in the early 19th century, it was restored and eventually, at the beginning of the 20th century, it became the modern nation of Saudi Arabia.

WEST AFRICA—UTHMAN DON FODIO

Another 18th-century reformer was Uthman Don Fodio (d. 1817), a scholar from the area of present-day Nigeria. Trained in Islamic law and theology, he criticized the rulers of his region. He accused them of

Islah and Tajdid

Two terms that were used a great deal by the reformers of the 18th and 19th centuries were *islah* ("reform") and *tajdid* ("renewal"). In their view reform and renewal were required if Islam was to be a vital force in the world.

The 18th-century reformers Wali Allah, Don Fodio, and al-Sanusi proposed a commitment to revitalize Muslim religion: to wage jihad, or striving on behalf of Islam. Jihad meant an individual struggle on the part of each Muslim to remain true to the principles of Islam. However it also meant an armed struggle in defense of Islam when this became necessary. When local rulers passed laws restricting the religious practices of the Muslim population Don Fodio declared jihad and with his followers he conquered a large region of West Africa. He established the state of Sokoto, run according to Islamic law, which survived until 1905. In Cyrenaica, part of what is today Libya, al-Sanusi also declared the need for jihad to establish a unified and strong faith among strongly independent Bedouin tribes (nomadic Arabs).

being unjust and tyrannical but also of allowing the local population to carry out rites involving magic and to mix the rituals and beliefs of Islam with the practices of other, local religions. He too called for a return to a pure Islamic faith.

INDIA—SHAH WALI ALLAH

Anger over the use of non-Islamic rituals by Muslims was shared by Shah Wali Allah (d. 1762), an Indian scholar. A member of the Naqshbandi order of the Sufis, he, unlike Ibn al-Wahhab, did not call for a ban on Sufism. Sufism was acceptable, even necessary, as long as the Sufis stayed true to Islam. He was particularly concerned with those who mixed Islamic and Hindu practices. He called for a renewed dedication of all Muslims to the Quran and hadith and the rejection of all foreign beliefs.

LIBYA—MUHAMMAD IBN AL-SANUSI

This spirit of reform carried outside cities and towns. In Cyrenaica, part of what is today Libya, Muhammad ibn Ali al-Sanusi (d. 1859) called for the purification of Sufism and Islam among Muslim Bedouins (nomadic Arabs). He established the Sanusi order of Sufism, pledged to asceticism and austerity in worship, in the Libyan desert oases, forming a strong coalition of Bedouin tribes dedicated to the true principles of Islam.

All these reform movements were centered on Islam and its need to reform and grow strong from within. Yet as successful as these measures were, Muslim society faced a growing threat from outside its territories: the increasing military and political power of Europe.

THE THREAT OF EUROPE

As the countries of Europe grew richer they began to cast a greedy eye on the regions of the Middle East, Asia, and Africa.

By the start of the 19th century wide regions of the Islamic world had fallen into the hands of European states. To many Muslims Islam itself was under attack.

In the 19th century Russia seized a vast area of Central Asia where the population was primarily Muslim, as it is today. The Dutch had seized Indonesia and parts of Malaysia. By 1911 they controlled both areas. It was the British and the French, however, who would rule over the largest parts of the Islamic world. By the early 19th century Britain controlled most of the Indian Peninsula and areas farther east in Southeast Asia. By the end of the century they had added Egypt and the Sudan to their empire. In the 1820s the French began sending troops against the regions of North Africa. Algeria fell first, around 1830, followed by Tunisia in 1881 and Morocco in 1912. Italy invaded the remaining area of North Africa (what is today Libya) in 1911.

The Ottomans were defeated and driven out of the Arab regions of the Middle East by Great Britain and by a widespread Arab revolt in northern Arabia and Syria during World War I (1914–18). Britain had promised to help the Arab regions achieve independence, but instead Britain and France decided in 1916 to carve up the Middle East between themselves. Britain seized a wide band of territory that included Palestine, Jordan, and Iraq, while the French took over the area that would later become Syria and Lebanon.

As a result, by the early 20th century the vast majority of the lands of Islam were European colonial states. In these regions Muslims now had very limited control over their political and economic lives. As the presence of the Europeans became greater it became clear that Muslims would have to accept drastic changes in their societies.

THE PENETRATION OF THE WEST

Colonial powers brought enormous changes to the lands they dominated. First they established European-style schools throughout the Islamic world. Students there learned European political and economic ideas as well as European approaches to science and technology. As students graduated and entered the labor market they carried these ideas into society at large. Second the colonial powers changed economic and business practices in Muslim regions. Commerce and production now benefited the Europeans rather than the local regions. Traditional merchants were forced out of business while a new generation of traders with strong ties to European trade arose.

THE ISLAMIC WORLD IN CRISIS

Over time, as those schooled in European ways gained wealth and power, they spread their practices to wider groups. Many Muslims were ready to accept the new ideas; others were suspicious of the changes being introduced into Islamic society. However regardless of what values they held most Muslims agreed that the Islamic world was in crisis. They faced disturbing questions of how Muslims were to react to the presence of the Europeans and what values and ideas Muslims would carry into the future. At stake was the future of Islam and Islamic society.

The conservative ulama and their supporters called for a rejection of European values and institutions. They called on Muslims to commit themselves more fully to the principles of Islam. Only then, they argued, would the Islamic community regain its unity and be able to compete with European states.

ADAPTATION AND REVITALIZATION

Other Muslims felt this attitude was too conservative. They agreed that it was important to defend Islam. However they argued that for the Islamic world to compete with the European states, it would have to adapt. They accused the ulama of living in the past and of not recognizing that Islamic law and education had to be reshaped if Muslims were to meet the

Young Muslim boys among the crowd gathered to hear speakers at the start of a London protest march against cartoons of the prophet Muhammad that were printed in a Danish newspaper. Anger over the cartoons created widespread outrage in Muslim communities internationally.

challenges of the modern world. These critics felt that rather than reject everything European, Muslims should use those ideas and institutions from Europe that could help revitalize Islamic society.

REFORMERS OF ISLAM

Many of the reform-minded Muslims took a strong interest in Western scientific ideas. They proposed that such ideas be incorporated into Islamic education. Science would thus open the way in the Islamic world to new military and scientific technologies, which would benefit the society as a whole.

CREATING A MODERN CODE OF RULES AND LAWS

Such reformers as Jamal al-Din al-Afghani (d. 1897), Muhammad Abduh (d. 1905), and Rashid Rida (d. 1935) looked for ways to adapt Islam to modern times. In Islam, they argued, lay all of the principles necessary to create a modern Islamic world. They agreed that the rituals of Islam and the guidance of the sharia were essential to Muslim life, but they believed that if the sharia was to deal with the problems of modem Islamic society it would have to be updated. This meant using the main principles of the sharia to create a modern code of rules and laws. Only a new and revitalized sharia, they declared, could put Islamic society back on its feet.

Many of these ideas were shared by two other leading Muslim thinkers of the late 19th and early 20th centuries: Sayyid Ahmad Khan (d. 1898) and later Muhammad Iqbal (d. 1938). Iqbal, a lawyer, admired European democracy and parliamentary government. He did not believe however that Muslims needed to borrow these ideas from Europe. Like al-Afghani he felt that these ideas were contained in the principles of the sharia and that Muslims needed only to reinterpret the sharia to reveal them.

RISE OF NATIONALISM

Although their writings would influence generations after them, Abduh, Iqbal, and the others never became politically powerful. For one thing their thinking attracted mostly students and intellectuals—not the broad population of Muslims. In addition they faced opposition from other Muslim thinkers. On one side the conservative ulama rejected the use of all European ideas and institutions, believing that such ideas were outside Islam. On the other side a new generation of Muslims felt comfortable with European political and economic ideas. This second group included those who embraced the idea of nationalism—the notion that a people should govern themselves and determine their own future without influence from foreign powers. It was an idea that would change the face of the Islamic world over the course of the 20th century.

TURKEY

As the 20th century progressed European rule over the Islamic world gave way to independent states. In 1923 Turkey—which was one of the few areas in the Islamic world never to have fallen under European rule—was declared an independent republic. The leader of the Turkish nationalist movement, Mustafa Kemal Ataturk (d. 1938), immediately set out to make Turkey a fully secularized (non-religious) state. The sharia was replaced by a European-style code of law; Muslim dress and customs were banned. Today Turkey remains the most secularized country of the Islamic world. In 1993 Tansu Ciller, leader of the True Path Party, became Turkey's prime minister, making her the third Muslim woman to be elected head of state, after Benazir Bhutto (d. 2007) in Pakistan and Khaleda Zia in Bangladesh. Today Turkey continues to strive for a balance between the political forces of secularism and Islam.

THE IDEA OF NATIONALISM

Nationalist ideas were spread by Muslim students who had been educated in European schools. These included both schools that had been established in Muslim regions and the universities in Europe itself at which Muslim youths studied. As new generations of Muslim students graduated the idea of nationalism caught on throughout the Islamic world.

PARLIAMENTARY SYSTEMS AND SECULAR UNIVERSITIES

The concept of nationalism gave rise to a number of political movements, all aimed at ending European colonialism. Their leaders usually included young Western-educated lawyers, journalists, and engineers. Earlier reformers had been committed to reforming Islamic law and education, but these young nationalists were less interested in religion. They did not hesitate to use ideas from Europe.

They campaigned for the creation of European-style political, legal, and educational institutions. Among the institutions they hoped to create in the Islamic world were parliamentary systems and secular (non-religious) universities.

Devout Muslims, and especially the ulama, received these ideas with skepticism. They were angry that the nationalists seemed to have set aside their commitment to Islam. Most of the nationalists felt that religion should be left out of politics. They were not against religious practices and beliefs but they felt that these had no place in the fight for independence.

GROWTH OF INDEPENDENT STATES

Soon after Turkey declared itself an independent republic, independence followed for other regions in the Islamic world: Iraq in 1932; Syria in 1947; Indonesia in 1950; Egypt in 1952; Morocco, Tunisia, and the Sudan in 1956; Malaysia in 1957; Nigeria in 1960; and, following a long and costly revolution, Algeria in 1962.

Pakistan came into being in 1947 in the midst of India's fight for independence from England. An Islamic nationalist movement, the Muslim League, had won support among the Muslims of India for a separate Muslim state. The League was finally able to create the state of Pakistan, but only after a civil war with India in which hundreds of thousands of Muslims and Hindus lost their lives. In 1971 the eastern half of Pakistan broke away after another bloody civil war to become Bangladesh.

THE STRUGGLE FOR POWER

In the majority of the newly independent Muslim states political power was held by secular governments. Many were controlled by military officers with no interest in combining religion and politics. This set the stage for conflict between the secular nationalists and the various groups within their states that supported Islamic forms of government. For these groups it was time to return to Islamic principles and the rule of the sharia.

Two such groups were the Society of Muslim Brothers, founded in Egypt in 1929 by Hasan al-Banna, and the Jamaat-i Islami, founded in India in 1941 by Mawlana Mawdudi. For both al-Banna and Mawdudi Islamic society was under attack not only by the European colonial powers but also by the secular nationalist movements. They savagely criticized these movements for adopting Western ideas and for abandoning Islam.

RELIGIOUS AND POLITICAL AGGITATION

For both leaders the separation of religion and politics was a violation of Islamic principles. They argued that Islam brought together all aspects of life, including politics and religion. Mawdudi, al-Banna, and others like them won the support of large numbers of Muslims. Unlike many of the ulama, they were dedicated to political activity. Their commitment to the faith struck a chord in the hearts of many Muslims over the first half of the 20th century.

The support these groups enjoyed did not escape the attention of the political leaders of the Islamic nations. Often their first reaction was to clamp down on these Islamic movements, sending their leaders to prison. Eventually however some leaders of Muslim states began to take a different approach. They tried to use religion to win the support of the broad population. In Egypt, the government of Jamal Abd al-Nasir (d. 1970) sponsored a religious newspaper and called for the support of the ulama of the Al-Azhar mosque. Al-Nasir's successor, Anwar Sadat (d. 1980), went even further in associating his government with religious symbols, events, and institutions such as al-Azhar. In Syria Hafiz al-Assad (d. 2000), who seized power in Egypt in 1970, repeatedly used Islam in this way in the 1970s and 1980s.

Sultana Ali, originally from Bangladesh, being sworn in as a U.S. citizen during Naturalization Ceremonies at the Onondaga Courthouse in Syracuse, New York.

GROWING SOCIAL AND ECONOMIC PROBLEMS

These gestures toward Islam, however, did little to change the unpopularity of the governments. Although these governments called themselves democratic, they ruled with little popular support and were also responsible for poor economic policies and rampant corruption. There were growing social problems, among them high rates of poverty and crime. To many devout Muslims the obvious reason for these problems was the decline of Islamic values and practices.

A NEW COMMITMENT TO ISLAM

In the late 1960s and early 1970s, as political, social, and economic problems continued to grow, Muslims throughout the Islamic world began to renew their commitment to Islam. There was a growing sense that Muslims should look to their own traditions and use them to revitalize their societies. Some now began to share the opinion that Islam—and particularly the sharia—contained all the guidance needed by individuals and society.

The new dedication to Islam took different forms. Many ordinary Muslims made a greater commitment to the beliefs and practices of Islam, and many began to lead what was seen as a more Islamic lifestyle. This included studying the Quran; carrying out daily prayer practices and the fast of Ramadan faithfully; supporting institutions such as clinics, schools, and youth centers run by religious organizations; and adopting modest styles of dress and public behavior. In cities and towns throughout the Islamic world it became more common to see young women wearing plain, long dresses and scarves over their hair.

THE MODERN WOMAN

The issue of the role of women is very complex in modern-day Islam. In areas that have undergone a fundamentalist movement or return to traditional ways, such as Afghanistan or Iran, the role of women has been curtailed in comparison with a few decades ago. In some places women are no longer allowed to study or to work. Their status is very difficult and oppression and brutality are a mark of these societies. In other areas such as Saudi Arabia, where women have been strictly constrained, small signs of change are seen, for example in allowing women to drive. However in most Muslim societies, women are encouraged to play a significant role in society but are also expected to dress modestly and behave appropriately. Overall, the last 30 years or so has seen a shift in how women dress and in their expectations. It is true to say that conforming to traditional dress and role codes has increased significantly, though whether that has seriously restricted the role women play within Muslim societies is an open discussion. To outsiders it looks more conservative but to those inside it is a return to traditional dress but with some modern ideas.

However for many Muslims the commitment to Islam was more than a return to Islamic ways. It was a call to political action. Across the Islamic world young Muslim men and women joined or formed political movements. Their message was that the time had come to put an end to secularized, Western-style governments and to make the sharia the foundation of Islamic society.

THE ISLAMIC REVOLUTION

Probably no single event in the mid-20th century had as much impact on the minds of Muslims as the 1979 Islamic Revolution in Iran. The revolution was carried out by a broad coalition made up of ulama, student groups, leftist organizations, and others—and was supported by many ordinary Iranians. Its goal was the overthrow of Shah Muhammad Reza Pahlavi (d. 1980).

The voice of the revolutionary movement was Ayatollah Khomeini (d. 1989), a religious scholar. Khomeini had harshly criticized the shah's policies as contrary to the teachings of Islam. Many Iranians were drawn to Khomeini's powerful religious message. He attacked the shah for undermining Islam with secularism and for his assault on the powers of the ulama. For his criticism Khomeini was arrested and sent into exile.

OVERTHROW OF THE SHAH

From exile Khomeini called for the overthrow of the shah and the creation of an Islamic-style government headed by the ulama. He argued that because the ulama were trained in Islamic law and theology, they were the only ones who could properly lead an Islamic government and society. In the fall of 1978 revolution broke out, and in early 1979 the shah fled the country. Khomeini returned in that year to Tehran and became the spiritual head of the Islamic Republic.

The effect of the revolution on the rest of the Islamic world was electric. For the first time an Islamic movement had successfully opposed a modern secular government. For many Muslims—particularly the new activists—the Islamic Revolution was enormously encouraging. It was a sign that a return to the ideals of Islam and the duties of the sharia could bring success. It also confirmed what Muslims could accomplish through political action.

The initial burst of enthusiasm for Khomeini and the Islamic Revolution gradually died away. The majority of the Sunni world did not fully accept Khomeini, a Shii leader, so relations with other Muslim countries suffered. Moreover the new Islamic government of Iran soon became as undemocratic as the shah's government had been. People who had grown accustomed to secular freedoms chafed under strict Islamic rule. Music was banned, women were forced to wear the burqa (a garment covering the face and body), and other freedoms were strictly curtailed.

ELECTION OF A MODERATE GOVERNMENT

By the mid-1990s Iran was suffering under economic hardships. People began to call for more progressive economic policies. In 1998 Iranians elected a moderate president, Muhammad Khatami. The outcome was a victory for the many women and young people who had voted for reform, rejecting conservative policies such as the dress code and other restrictive regulations.

In the spirit of reform Iran appointed its first female senior judge, and freedom of speech improved. Muslim authorities lifted the ban on women leading congregational prayers for other women, which had been a problem in all-girl schools. Iran's more moderate government took steps toward improving relations with Europe and the United States and saw its relationships with other Muslim countries improve as well.

Although some heartening political adjustments have been made since the Islamic Revolution was waged more than 25 years ago, recent tensions over Iran's alleged efforts to develop nuclear weapons have reduced any visible advances to a trivial level. Worries grow among many Muslim and non-Muslim countries that Iran might become the first nuclear theocracy (a form of government in which a god or deity is recognized as the supreme civil ruler).

THE BALKAN CRISIS

At about the same time as the Islamic revolution in Iran, in Eastern Europe a rise in Serb nationalism proved disastrous for Muslims in the former Yugoslavia. After the death of the Communist leader Josip Broz Tito in 1980 the ethnic groups that had made up Yugoslavia began to break apart along nationalist lines: Serb, Croat, and Muslim. The strongest of these were the Serbs, with dreams of a "Greater Serbia" that would reunite all of the lands that had historically been Serbian. Although they were concentrated in Bosnia, Muslims were not a majority there although they were in the majority in Kosovo, an autonomous federal unit in Yugoslavia which was stripped of its autonomy in 1989. Muslims had always tried to live peacefully beside their neighbors but now found themselves caught in the midst of a war not of their making.

In March 1994 Muslims and Croats in Bosnia signed an agreement that created Bosnia and Herzegovina as an independent state. This did not ensure their safety, however. In spite of United Nations (UN) peacekeeping efforts, in July 1995 the Serb army attacked Srebrenica, a Muslim "safe area." They took the Muslim men to a field outside the town and shot them. Srebrenica thus became the site of the worst massacre of civilians in Europe since World War II (1939–45). Exactly how many Muslim men died may never be known but the numbers were horrific. The event brought a new phrase into the English language: "ethnic cleansing."

The Dayton Peace Accords of 1995 ended the war but not the hatred. Thousands of Muslims were left homeless, unable to return to towns where hostility still runs high. In addition many Muslim homes were seized by Serbs or burned to prevent their owners from reclaiming them. The massacre also left thousands of widows and fatherless children whose only offense was to be Muslim.

The bridge at Mostar in the Republic of Montenegro. This famous bridge was built by an Ottoman architect in 1566 and destroyed in 1993 after being bombarded by tank fire during the Bosnian conflict. After the war ended, the bridge was rebuilt and opened again in 2004.

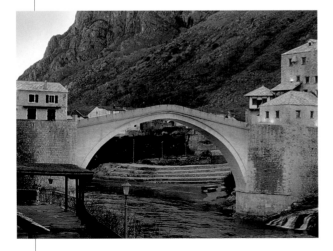

Bosnia is not the only region in which Muslims suffered tremendous losses. When Yugoslavia was breaking up, Kosovo, a region of Serbia that was originally part of Albania, wanted its independence. People in Kosovo were more than 80 percent Muslim. Serbia sent troops into Kosovo to put down revolutionary activity. Waves of refugees fled to neighboring countries. In 1998 Serbian troops killed many of the civilian inhabitants of Drenica, a hilly region in central Kosovo, mostly Muslim women and children. Following the conflict, Kosova technically remained part of Serbia although it was under UN jurisdiction. Kosova unilaterally declared its indepdenence from Serbia in February 2008 which has been followed by recognition from many UN states.

THE MIDDLE EAST

The establishment of Israel as a nation in 1948 left many Palestinian Arabs without a homeland. Muslim and Christian Arabs were displaced from a land they had inhabited for centuries. Their plight was largely unnoticed by the Western nations until the 1967 war between Israel and the Arab states of Egypt, Syria, and Jordan. In a few short days the three Arab armies met defeat. In the process Jerusalem—sacred to Jews, Christians, and Muslims—was completely taken over by the Israelies.

Over the next 20 years relations among countries in the Middle East stabilized somewhat. The Palestinians however still suffered under Israeli rule, watching Israeli settlers claim lands that had been theirs. Beginning in 1987 the Palestinians began to assert themselves politically, and at times with arms, in what was called the "uprising," or intifada, under Yasir Arafat until his death in November 2004. Continued acts of resistance have drawn attention to the Palestinian cause and eventually brought the Israelis and the Palestinians to the bargaining table.

Many issues remain unresolved between Israel and the Palestinians. One is Jerusalem, the location of the Dome of the Rock and al-Aqsa Mosque, from which the prophet ascended to heaven. Devout Muslims call for its liberation from Israel as well as for a separate Palestinian state.

In 2005 Israel withdrew from the Gaza Strip after 38 years of occupation and dismantled all of its settlements, providing hope that a Palestinian state may be a possibility for the future. Yet the early 2006 parliamentary elections won by the radical Hamas party in Palestine have raised tensions and tempered hope, as has the building by Israel of a wall dividing Israel from Palestine and creating an economic embargo on many areas of Palestine.

AFGHANISTAN: THE TALIBAN

After the breakup of the Soviet Union in 1992 former Soviet countries such as Afghanistan, Azerbaijan, Turkmenistan, Uzbekistan, and Tajikistan, previously secular and Communist, have emerged with growing Islamic identities. Only in Afghanistan, however, has there been a move toward a purely Islamic state.

The Soviet Union had tried to impose Communist rule from 1979 until 1989; this was disastrous for Afghanistan. In many ways the Western powers, especially the United States, played a game of proxy war with the Soviet forces by funding and arming Islamic resistance fighters. As a result the Russians were driven out of Afghanistan but this left a massive power vacuum into which poured Western-armed and -funded warlords. Afghanistan descended into anarchy and many longed for a strong leadership to emerge to curb the warlords.

A Muslim woman wearing a burqa in northern Afghanistan. The burqa is usually made of lightweight material that has two layers. This gives Muslim women the opportunity to reveal or completely cover their eyes. In some Muslim societies it is normal practice for women to be fully covered and religious or cultural tradition may govern dress codes. In other societies, dress codes may vary and some women dress modestly, usually covering their heads, arms, and legs while others may choose to wear garments or cloaks that cover the body more fully.

THE TALIBAN

In 1994 a new group made up mostly of Afghani religious students burst onto the world scene. They called themselves the Taliban. They announced that their mission was to free Afghanistan from its corrupt leadership and to create a society in accord with Islam. A strong and well-trained fighting force, they lost no time in taking control.

By 1998 the Taliban had come close to its goal of unifying Afghanistan under its rule. However its fundamentalist interpretation of Islamic law created new problems. A ban on women's employment fell with unequal force on widows and their children—barred from working, female heads of households faced starvation. The UN criticized the Taliban's restrictions not only on women's employment but also on education and health care, and it suspended aid.

OSAMA BIN LADEN

The Taliban also harbored Osama bin Laden the leader of the terrorist organization al-Qaeda, which attacked New York and Washington on September 11, 2001. The United States and its allies invaded Afghanistan and ousted the Taliban. Three years later in December 2004 Hamid Karzai was sworn in as Afghanistan's first popularly elected president. The new constitution and parliamentary elections also showed the changes in relation to Islam. President Karzai used this election result as an example to underscore his claim that democracy and Islam are compatible. However the continued power of the Taliban and the return of warlords have left much of Afghanistan in a state of war.

ISLAM IN EUROPE

Approximately 14 million Muslims are found in western Europe, with the vast majority in France (5.5 million), Germany (3.5 million), England (1.8 million), the Netherlands (500,000), and Belgium (300,000). Many came as workers to make up for the short supply of manpower in these countries in the 1950s and 1960s.

Muslims who have lived in Europe for generations may still find life there a difficult fit. One reason is that many Muslims have been denied settled immigrant status; those born in Germany, for example, are not automatically granted citizenship. Many still suffer marginalization, unemployment, and poverty, and many have complained about police harassment and other forms of abuse. European countries, which have traditionally identified with Christianity, have viewed with suspicion attempts by the young Muslim generation to assert their own religious and cultural identity. A problem for many European Muslims, then, is to find a form of Islam that fits their new identities as Europeans who are Muslims—entering into European society while preserving their Islamic way of life.

ISLAM IN THE UNITED STATES

In the mid-1970s 800,000 people, or 0.4 percent of the American population, identified themselves as Muslims. In the mid-1990s the number had swelled to 3,560,000, and by 2008 it was estimated that there were between 7 and 8 million Muslims. Numbers vary according to different sets of data and the figure may be even higher. These numbers include people born into the religion, immigrants to America who have brought their Islamic beliefs with them, and converts who may be Caucasian, African American, Hispanic, or even Native American.

The Islamic community exercises increasing influence in American life. One area in which Muslim influence may be seen is in education. American Muslims have long emphasized the importance of educating young people in the ethics and beliefs of Islam so as to equip them to lead morally responsible lives. To Muslims this emphasis on moral responsibility is important for two reasons: first to offer a clear alternative to Muslim young people in American society, and second to demonstrate to Americans at large the stress Muslims place on living morally and ethically.

Thanks to a greater awareness of Muslims as a presence in America Muslim students enrolled at American colleges and universities gradually experienced greater acceptance. This experience underwent a serious jolt, however, on September 11, 2001, with the deadly destruction of the terrorists' attacks on the World Trade Center in New York and the Pentagon in Washington. In the following months, many foreign Muslim students in the United States

NATION OF ISLAM

A growing group among the Muslims of America is the Nation of Islam. An American movement now under the leadership of Louis Farrakhan, it has more than 1.6 million followers. Mainstream Muslims generally say that the Nation is not part of the Islamic community. They find many of the Nation's teachings, particularly those about other races and religions, to be out of step with traditional Islam, which recognizes all people and all races to be equal before God. In recent years however the Nation has shown signs of change in ways that may bring it more into line with orthodox Islam.

returned to their homelands out of fear of reprisals against them. Many American Muslims keenly felt the suspicions against them that these events raised in the minds of their fellow citizens.

THE WAR IN IRAQ

The two most significant historical events of recent years that have focused attention on the Muslim world have been the terrorist attacks on the United States on September 11, 2001, and the war in Iraq. The United States justified its invasion of Iraq on March 16, 2003, primarily by a focus on Saddam Hussein, a brutal dictator, and the possibility that he might have weapons of mass destruction that could be used in further terrorist attacks on the United States and throughout the world. The war has brought a heightened awareness of the religious complexity of that Muslim country and Islam in general.

The majority of the Iraqi population are Shiis who felt persecuted under the Sunni-dominated rule of Saddam Hussein. For the Kurds, who are mostly Sunnis, their goal for an autonomous Kurdish region takes priority over any alliance with their fellow non-Kurdish Sunnis. As a minority the Sunnis fear that democracy will not be in their favor, so they have joined the political process only reluctantly. Attempts to reconfigure post-Hussein Iraq could lead to political dominance of the Shii majority; a religiously neutral society respecting all forms of Islamic belief; a Shii theocracy; a coalition government; or a civil war.

No matter what the results in the near future, the situation will be tense for many years to come and will affect the religious and civil life of other Muslim nations, especially Iran, Syria, Turkey, Afghanistan, Bahrain, and Lebanon. Combined with the unstable situation in Afghanistan and the earlier failures in the Balkans, this war, considered by many to be illegal, has given rise to the perception by many

An American soldier patrols the streets on the outskirts of Sadr City in Iraq. The events that have unfolded in the country highlight the religious and political complexity that exists in Iraq.

Muslims and Westerners alike that the West wishes to destroy the power of Islam.

ISLAM FACING THE 21ST CENTURY

As the Islamic world has moved into the 21st century, it has looked back on three centuries of struggle. Beginning in the 18th century Muslim culture lost much of its vitality as its political and economic power gave way to Europe's greater technological and military might. Europe's march through the Islamic world continued through the 19th and early 20th centuries. During that time Islamic thinkers tried to understand the reasons for Europe's dominance and to find ways for Islam to adapt to the new ideas that were entering the culture from the West. Their soul-searching gave rise to a nationalism that blended the religious and legal culture of Islam with notions of independence and enabled them to throw off European dominance. Today the Islamic world holds a stronger position in the world than at any time since the 18th century.

EMERGENCE OF PAN-ISLAM

Increasingly identity within Muslim countries is as strongly defined by religion as it is by the nation. The emergence of Pan-Islam (a political movement promoting the unity of Muslims under one Islamic state) is becoming a major factor in world affairs. One example is the massive growth in Islamic banking that started in 1975 and now manages more than $300 billion in assets. This movement sought to challenge the norms of conventional banking and to find ways in which Muslims could trade, bank, and invest in accordance with Islamic teachings. Its success indicates not only the rise of a Muslim middle class worldwide, but also a desire to be rooted in tradition. The Pan-Islam trend is also reflected in other spheres such as the growth of media in Muslim countries—for example the Al Jazeera TV network, which rivals the BBC and CNN in international coverage but from an avowedly Muslim perspective. Pan-Islam is also reflected in the multinational makeup of some of the extreme groups that draw fighters from many countries, united by their support of violence as a means to Islamic victory.

BRIDGING A RISING DIVIDE

Many in both the West and Muslim lands emphasize a divide between Western values and Islamic values. However, others say that this divide is one largely of ignorance and fear and can be bridged by seeking common ground and building friendships.

One effort in this direction was a letter written by nearly 140 Muslim leaders in 2007 to Christian leaders seeking to explore areas of common concern such as the environment, international relationships, and mutual understanding; such a letter would have been unimaginable only a few years earlier.

Despite these major developments, for most Muslims Islam continues to be what it has always been: a stable rock of certainty; a moral code; and a place of friendship, mutual support, and relationship with God in the midst of the tempests of the world.

Many Muslims today have grown up in a secular world. As they look around them they see a society full of problems—including unemployment, crime, and declining moral values. Like generations of young people before them they are looking for new approaches, new ways to order their lives in a difficult world. Islam for them is one such way. Always renewing itself, it offers them a real alternative for change. The force of the Islamic revival sweeping the world today is the force of youth, with its belief that the world can become a better place.

AN ETERNAL QUEST

Islam is by its very nature an endless revolution, an eternal quest to reach out to God. Muslims are committed to challenge what they see as wrong. They may not be passive. Whatever happens the future of Islam will include a great deal of debate and perhaps even conflict. Although activism seems on the rise, most in the Muslim world oppose militancy and extremism or feel that the sharia should not be the basis of government. It seems most likely that Islam will remain a religion and civilization that encompasses a variety of points of view. This was true of Islam early in its history and it remains true today.

FACT FILE

Worldwide numbers
The Islamic faith has more than 1.4 billion followers.

Holy Symbol
The star and crescent; some Muslims say that the Islamic faith guides a person, in the same way that the moon and stars guide a traveler. Some Islamic states have this symbol on their flag.

Festivals
Ramadan, a month-long festival, is the most important. It marks the time when the Quran was revealed to Muhammad and the gates of hell were closed and the gates of heaven were opened to him. Ramadan is the ninth month of the Muslim calendar. Id al-Fitr marks the end of Ramadan, when thanks is given to Allah for helping with the fasting. It is also seen as a time of renewed commitment to the faith. Another festival, Id al-Adha, marks the time when prophet Abraham was willing to sacrifice his son at God's command.

Holy Writings
The main holy writing in the Islamic faith is the Quran. Many Muslims believe that the Quran was written by God before time began and was then revealed to the prophet Muhammad. The Quran is written and recited in Arabic.

Holy Places
The most important holy place for Muslims is Mecca in Saudia Arabia because it is the birthplace of the prophet Muhammad. It is also special because the mosque in Mecca contains the Kaaba, worshipped as the first house of God on earth. All Muslims try at least once in their lives to make the pilgrimage to Mecca. The cities of Medina and Jerusalem are also regarded as holy.

Founders
It is believed that the Islamic faith has been slowly revealed to humanity through a number of different prophets. However the final revelation was given to the prophet Muhammad in the seventh century C.E. Many have a great amount of respect for Muhammad and will usually add the words "peace be upon him" after speaking or writing his name, but it is only God that is worshipped.

BIBLIOGRAPHY

An-Na`im Abdullahi Ahmed. *Islam and the Secular State: Negotiating the Future of Shari'a.* Mass.: Harvard University Press, 2008.

Newsweek magazine. Available online. URL: http://www. newsweek.com/. News and statistics on Muslims in the United States and worldwide.

Nigosian, Solomon Alexander. *Islam: Its History, Teaching, and Practices.* Bloomington: Indiana University Press, 2004.

Richardson, Joel. *Antichrist: Islam's Awaited Messiah.* Enumclaw, Wash.: Pleasant Word-A Division of WinePress Publishing, 2006.

FURTHER READING

Ahmed, Akbar S. *Journey into Islam: The Crisis of Globalization.* Washington D.C.: Brookings Institution Press, 2007.

Ayoub, Mahmoud. *Islam: Faith and History.* Oxford: Oneworld, 2004.

Breuilly, Elizabeth, and O'Brien Joanne, and Palmer, Martin. *Religions of the World.* New York: Checkmark Books, 2005.

Brown, Daniel W. *A New Introduction to Islam.* Malden, Mass.: Blackwell Publishing, 2004.

Campo, Juan E. *Encyclopedia of Islam.* New York: Facts On File, 2009.

DeLong-Bas, Natana. *Wahhabi Islam: From Revival and Reform to Global Jihad.* Oxford and New York: Oxford University Press, 2004.

Dunn, John. *The Spread of Islam.* San Diego, Calif.: Lucent Books, 1996.

Esposito, John L., and Mogahed, Dalia. *Who Speaks For Islam?: What a Billion Muslims Really Think.* Washingtion D.C.: Gallup Press, 2008.

Irwin, Robert. *Islamic Art in Context.* New York: Harry N. Abrams, Inc., 1997.

Marshall, Paul A. *Islam at the Crossroads.* Grand Rapids, Mich.: Baker Books, 2002.

Nasr, Seyyed Hossein. *A Young Muslim's Guide to the Modern World.* Chicago: Kazi Publications, Inc., 1994.

Ruthven, Malise. *Islam: A Very Short Introduction.* New York: Oxford University Press, 1997.

Swisher, Clarice, ed. *The Spread of Islam.* San Diego, Calif.: Greenhaven Press, 1998.

Weiss, Walter M. *Islam: An Illustrated Historical Overview.* Hauppauge, N.Y.: Barron's, 2000.

Wormser, Richard. *American Islam: Growing Up Muslim in America.* New York: Walter and Company, 2002.

WEB SITES

Further facts and figures, history, and current status of the religion can be found on the following Web sites:

www.islamworld.net
A site looking at the Muslim way of life.

www.religionfacts.com/islam/
A comprehensive summary of the faith from a site dealing with all major religions of the world.

www.bbc.co.uk/religion/religions/islam
A guide to Islam, including history, beliefs, holy days around the world, and message boards.

www.religioustolerance.org/islam.htm
This site contains balanced, clear, objective, and inclusive articles about religion, morality and ethics. It deals with Islam alongside other major faiths.

GLOSSARY

adhan—The call to prayer made five times daily from the minarets of mosques.

Allah—The Islamic term, derived from Arabic, meaning God.

aya—A verse of the Quran. Each chapter (*see* SURA) contains one or more of these verses.

baraka—Spiritual blessing. Used to refer to the powers of particularly religious individuals, such as "saints."

burqa—A garment covering the face and body.

caliph—Term deriving from the Arabic word *khalifa*. It was the title used by the rulers of the Islamic Empire. It can also mean "representative" or "deputy."

dhikr—"Remembrance" of God. Used by the Sufis to refer to their ritual practices.

ghazwa—Raid in the pre-Islamic period and in early Islam.

hadith—The collection of reports or a single report relating the words and deeds of the prophet Muhammad. The words and deeds themselves are known as the Sunna, or "way of acting."

hajj—Pilgrimage, specifically to Mecca. The annual pilgrimage is held in the month of Dhu al-Hijja and is one of the Five Pillars of Islam.

Hijra—"Emigration." The term used to refer to the journey by the prophet Muhammad and his companions from Mecca to Medina in 622.

Id al-Adha—The annual feast day of sacrifice held on the 10th day of the Islamic month Dhu al-Hijja, the month of pilgrimage.

Id al-Fitr—The annual festival in which the end of the month of fasting, Ramadan, is celebrated.

ihram—The white garments worn by pilgrims in Mecca during the annual pilgrimage (*see* HAJJ). These garments are also indicative of ritual purity.

imam—Used by Muslims to refer to the leader of a session of prayer or a religious teacher. The Shia use the term for special individuals viewed as the religious and political leaders of the community.

Islam—An Arabic word meaning to submit or surrender, specifically to the will of God.

jami—The congregational mosque used particularly though not only on Fridays for the weekly sermon and noon prayer.

jihad—"Striving" for one's religion. Often translated as "holy war."

khutba—The sermon, usually by a prominent religious figure, given in the congregational mosque at the Friday noon prayer session.

kuttab—Quranic school usually attended before the start of regular schooling.

Mahdi—The messianic figure who it is believed will arrive at the end of time to bring justice and order to the world.

masjid—A local or neighborhood mosque. *see* JAMI.

mawlid—The festival commemorating the birthday of a religious figure, usually a "saint." Another term used is *musim*.

muadhdhin—Or muezzin. The individual who makes the call to prayer (*see* ADHAN) five times daily from the minaret of a mosque.

Muslim—A believer of Islam; anything pertaining to the religion, law, or culture of Islam.

qadi—Judge in a sharia court, usually appointed by the state.

qibla—The direction of Mecca in which all Muslims must pray. In mosques it is indicated by the *mihrab*, or prayer niche, found in every mosque.

sadaqa—Voluntary almsgiving.

salat—Prayer. One of the Five Pillars of Islam.

sawm—Fasting, particularly the annual fast of Ramadan. One of the Five Pillars of Islam.

shahada—Bearing witness to the oneness of God and to the prophethood of Muhammad. Also one of the Five Pillars of Islam.

sharia—The system of law in Islam based on the Quran and Muhammad's sunna. Often translated as "holy law."

shaykh—Elderly man, teacher, or tribal leader. Also the head of a Sufi organization or center.

shirk—Associating any object *or* being with God. The one unforgivable sin of Islam.

sura—A chapter of the Quran.

taaziya—Passion play held each year in Shii communities to commemorate the death of Husayn ibn Ali.

tafsir—Interpretation, usually of the Quran.

tariqa—A Sufi order.

tawaf—Ritual circling of the Kaaba in Mecca that is part of the annual pilgrimage for Muslims.

ulama—Religious and legal experts.

umma—Community, specifically a religious community. Most often used in Islam to refer to the Islamic community.

wudu—Ritual cleansing performed before each session of prayer.

zakat—Legal almsgiving considered obligatory for Muslims and calculated on the basis of income. One of the Five Pillars of Islam.

INDEX